KNOWLEDGE BASED MANAGEMENT

A SYSTEMATIC APPROACH TO ENHANCED BUSINESS PERFORMANCE AND STRUCTURED INNOVATION

PRAISE FOR *KNOWLEDGE BASED MANAGEMENT*

"Air Academy's new book, Knowledge Based Management, is excellent for executives trying to lead change in their companies. It describes the evolution and continued improvement in thinking from Deming, Juran and Ishikawa to Six Sigma, Lean Manufacturing and Design for Six Sigma. The recommended questions that leaders must ask their organizations are especially helpful, and the overview of DFSS is the best I have seen."

M. David Jones
President and CEO
Stanadyne Corporation

"The value proposition of Air Academy's new Knowledge Based Management text is its ability to help us sustain the gains by teaching extremely effective and easy-to-learn principles of process improvement. As a direct result, we reduced rework in one major area from 50% to less than 1% of WIP within six months, became nearly debt free in six years, increased our stock from under $4 to over $20 per share, provided our people with great career opportunities and created growth that is far outpacing our competition. Thank you, Air Academy."

Russ Huffer
Chairman and CEO
Apogee Enterprises, Inc

"Air Academy's text, Knowledge Based Management, represents an extremely practical and essential primer for those involved in leading enterprise-wide performance improvement. I highly recommend it for every business executive."

Kenn Lendrum
Vice-President GMS Canada
GlaxoSmithKline

"The speed of improvement for any organization is gated by its ability to rapidly solve problems. The application of systematic problem solving tools is gained only through cycles of learning. AAA has done an excellent job of condensing their cycles of experience into a text that provides the roadmap for maturing an organization's ability to make application of powerful problem solving techniques thereby increasing the velocity of improvement."

Russell W. Ford
President/CEO
Prestolite Electric, Inc.

PRAISE FOR *KNOWLEDGE BASED MANAGEMENT*

"The authors of Knowledge Based Management have gotten it right. Delivering superior value to customers along with the capability and passion for improving everything internally are key determinants of business success. This exciting new text provides us the philosophy and tools to do just that."

James D. Wiggins
Operating Principal
Kohlberg & Company

"This book is the most comprehensive, practical guide to driving operational excellence through easy-to-understand concepts and quantitative methods. The author's "Keep It Simple Statistically" (KISS) approach to solving complex business issues will inspire the reader to develop and implement action plans that drive positive bottom line results."

Al Lanzetta
Senior Vice President, Operations and Global Services
Egenera, Inc.

"Some companies are good at execution, which allows them to be durable. Other companies are good at innovation, which allows them to be great. Implementing Lean Six Sigma and innovation together creates companies that are both durable and great. Knowledge Based Management and Air Academy's competitive excellence model helps companies set a course and start their journey to delighting customers, shareholders and employees alike."

Michael Cyger
CEO
iSixSigma

"Knowledge Based Management weaves decades of business improvement learning and knowledge into a concise, easy-to-read text. While some authors represent similar topics as unique and revolutionary methods, Air Academy Associates thread past, present and future thinking together as an integrated and holistic approach. The accumulated knowledge summarized in this book will be a significant value-add for any organization on the improvement journey, irregardless of maturity. Air Academy's "Keep It Simple Statistically" (KISS) approach not only yields real and rapid business improvements, it engages and motivates all who use it."

George Maszle
Director, Lean Six Sigma
Xerox Corporation

ABOUT THE AUTHORS

Mark J. Kiemele, President and Co-founder of Air Academy Associates, has more than 30 years of teaching, coaching and consulting experience. Having mentored more than 30,000 leaders, scientists, engineers, managers, trainers, practitioners, and college students from more than 20 countries, he is world-renowned for his Knowledge Based KISS (Keep It Simple Statistically) approach to engaging practitioners in applying statistical methods. Dr. Kiemele has been involved in the origin and evolution of Six Sigma, as he trained the first Six Sigma Black Belts at the Six Sigma Research Institute at Motorola and has helped deploy and implement Six Sigma at more than 60 companies worldwide. His support has been requested by an impressive list of global clients, including Xerox, Sony, Microsoft, GE, Raytheon, Lockheed-Martin, Northrop-Grumman, Woodward, Samsung, GlaxoSmithKline, PerkinElmer, Danaher, Corning, EMC, Kaiser Aluminum, General Dynamics Land Systems, Army Material Command, Apogee, Bose, Heritage Valley Health System, John Deere, Valeant, and Brunswick.

Dr. Kiemele earned a B.S. and M.S. in Mathematics from North Dakota State University and a Ph.D. in Computer Science from Texas A&M University. During his time in the U.S. Air Force, he supported the design, development and testing of various weapon systems, including the Maverick and Cruise Missile systems, and was a professor at the U.S. Air Force Academy. In addition to many published papers, he has co-authored the books *Basic Statistics: Tools for Continuous Improvement*; *Applied Modeling and Simulation: an Integrated Approach to Development and Operation*; *Network Modeling, Simulation, and Analysis*; and most recently *Lean Six Sigma: A Tools Guide*. He is also the editor of the text *Understanding Industrial Designed Experiments*.

Richard C. Murrow, CEO of Air Academy Associates, has over thirty years of management and leadership experience in complex and diversified organizations. As Vice President Quality Systems, GE Mortgage, Dr. Murrow trained and supported the business leaders, enhanced the business systems, and deployed the Six Sigma methodology. As Quality and Management Innovation Director, he orchestrated the creation of a Center of Excellence and provided the leadership for a nationally recognized Quality and Management Innovation Program. He also implemented operational improvements in performance systems throughout the USAF Air Combat Command, an organization of 165,000 employees at 32 main operating locations.

Dr. Murrow earned a B.S. in Aeronautical Engineering from USAF Academy, a M.S. in Astronautical Engineering from Purdue University, an MBA from Rensselaer Polytechnic Institute, and a PhD in Aerospace Engineering from University of Colorado. Since 1999, Dr. Murrow has worked directly with senior leadership, management, and quality directors of such leading companies as Sony, Hyundai, Gates Rubber, Raytheon, St. Jude Medical, Textron Financial Corporation, Shell, Lockheed Martin, GlaxoSmithKline, Bose, Grupo IMSA, Kimberly Clark, Samsung Capital, and multiple government departments and agencies to improve processes, products, services, and business systems.

Lee R. Pollock, Senior Vice-President of Air Academy Associates, has served for more than thirty years in design and systems engineering, test engineering, quality management, strategic planning and plant management. Since 2000, he has taught and mentored thousands of executives, managers, trainers and practitioners throughout the US and abroad on Knowledge Based Management. His list of clients include Lockheed Martin, Sony, GlaxoSmithKline, Perkin Elmer, Nova Chemicals, Gates Rubber, EMC, Raytheon, Lydall, Apogee Enterprises, Holley Performance, Stanadyne, Thilmany, Packaging Dynamics, Singer/SVP Worldwide, Bombardier, the US Army and Air Force.

Dr. Pollock earned a B.S. from the US Military Academy, M.S. in Engineering from Northeastern University and Ph.D. in Operations Research from the Florida Institute of Technology. He led the DOD charge introducing best commercial practices within militarized systems and spearheaded Electronic Systems Center's winning of the National Quality Award as presented by former President Bill Clinton. He also developed Air Academy's first course on Lean Six Sigma Initialization and Best Practices and co-authored *Lean Six Sigma: A Tools Guide*. Dr. Pollock continues to teach, mentor, write and market for Air Academy Associates.

OTHER TEXTS BY AIR ACADEMY ASSOCIATES

Understanding Industrial Designed Experiments

4th Edition, ISBN 1-880156-03-2

by Stephen R. Schmidt and Robert G. Launsby.

This is an applications oriented text which blends the competing Taguchi, Shainin, and classical approaches to designed experiments into a new and powerful approach for gaining knowledge. Rules of Thumb are emphasized to enable the reader to implement the techniques without being encumbered with mathematical complexity. Topics include: Full and Fractional Factorials, Plackett-Burman, Box-Behnken, Central Composite, D-optimal, Mixture, Nested and Robust Designs. Included are over 300 pages of actual industrial case studies from a wide variety of industries. Simulation software and the student version of the DOE KISS software package are also included.

Basic Statistics: Tools for Continuous Improvement

4th Edition, ISBN 1-880156-06-7

by Mark J. Kiemele, Stephen R. Schmidt, and Ronald J. Berdine.

This text provides a refreshingly new approach to applying statistical tools for moving up the performance improvement ladder. Emphasis is on "statistical thinking" for transforming data into information, plus applications. Topics include: Why Statistics; Steps Before Collecting Data; Descriptive Statistics; Probability Distributions; Confidence Intervals; Hypothesis Testing; Analysis of Variance; Regression; Design of Experiments; Statistical Process Control; Gage Capability; Multivariate Charts; Reliability; and Quality Function Deployment. More than 65 examples and case studies, contributed by more than 10 industrial practitioners, span manufacturing, service, software, government, and the health care industries. Included is the student version of SPC KISS, a very user friendly statistical applications software package.

Lean Six Sigma: A Tools Guide

2nd Edition, ISBN 1-880156-07-5

by Murray Adams, Mark Kiemele, Lee Pollock and Tom Quan

The Tools Guide is an easy to use reference guide for practitioners who are interested in improving the way they do business. It presents a host of Lean Six Sigma tools in the context of the DMAIC process improvement framework. Both transactional and manufacturing applications of the tools are presented. It presents Lean and Six Sigma as a synergistic force rather than two competing initiatives. This handbook was written for anyone involved in process improvement, including those who may not have received formal training in Lean or Six Sigma, a college degree or a background in statistics. It only requires a passion to make a difference.

INsourcing Innovation

ISBN 0-9769010-0-5

by David Silverstein, Neil DeCarlo and Michael Slocum

This book was written because most business leaders are dissatisfied with the ability of their companies to innovate. It provides a simple framework for thinking about business excellence and a roadmap for implementing structured innovation. It covers both the tactical and strategic aspects of TRIZ (The Theory of Inventive Problem Solving) focusing on the implementation methodology. There are several case studies included which show an in-depth breakdown of how TRIZ was used to create innovative solutions. Finally, it shows why structured innovation must be a key component of the larger system of total performance excellence and, at the same time, how other key aspects of business excellence enable structured innovation.

Knowledge Based Management

A Systematic Approach to Enhanced Business Performance and Structured Innovation

Second Edition

Mark J. Kiemele
Richard C. Murrow
Lee R. Pollock

AIR ACADEMY ASSOCIATES

Colorado Springs, Colorado

Library of Congress Catalog Card Number: 95-83869

ISBN-10: 1-880156-08-3

ISBN-13: 978-1-880156-08-7

Printed in the United States of America

2   – 08

Distributed by: Six Sigma Products Group, Inc.

1650 Telstar Drive, Suite 110

Colorado Springs, CO 80920

Production / Graphics: Douglas Vaughn, Air Academy Associates,
Colorado Springs, CO

The authors recognize that perfection is unattainable without continuous improvement. Therefore, we solicit comments as to how to improve this text. To relay your comments or to obtain further information, contact:

AIR ACADEMY ASSOCIATES, LLC
1650 Telstar Drive, Suite 110
Colorado Springs, CO 80920
Phone: (719) 531-0777 ♦ FAX: (719) 531-0778
e-mail: aaa@airacad.com
website: www.airacad.com

To our wives and families who have made many sacrifices as we continue our quest to build intellectual capital for the betterment of business; to preserve the useful, perfect the valuable, and promote a culture of continuous innovation.

Table of Contents

Foreword

Competitive Excellence is not a paradigm shift - it is a brave new world! The pressures the modern corporation faces are fierce, involving the need to preserve and evolve the business. Competitive Excellence is the successful integration of preservation and evolution with culture and infrastructure. This book establishes the vital information necessary to get this integration exactly right. The Questions Leaders Must Answer and The Questions Leaders Must Ask provide a framework for defining the need, identifying the method(s) to meet the need, and the successful application of the method(s) to satisfy the need. These questions extend the works of the quality gurus Deming, Juran, and Ishikawa to the modern era of mandated competitive excellence and innovation.

I recommend every leader read this book, because it contains a simple message that can help a company transform itself. It gives leaders something they can use immediately together with a vision for the future state of their business plus a roadmap to get there. The knowledge based approach presented in this book is the most clear-cut and straightforward approach I know to acquire and manage the knowledge needed to effectively maintain and evolve a business. It is enticingly simple yet profound.

Dr. Michael Slocum

Preface

The first edition of this book has had a long life. Frankly, we were surprised at the reception of such a simple but fundamental concept that the right kind of knowledge delivers performance improvement. The book's long life is due to the fact that it has been a foundation-builder for continuous improvement in many organizations. The concept of knowledge based management has not changed, but times have. The speed at which organizations must improve is at least an order of magnitude faster than what it was a decade ago. This second edition addresses the modern era of performance improvement and provides its readers with the best available strategies and methods to help their organizations become and remain competitive.

Any leader at any level who wants to improve his or her organization's bottom line will benefit from reading this text. We define a leader as anyone who is entrusted with resources and who is expected to use them wisely. This definition includes executive leadership, managers at every level, Belts of any color, and practitioners who exert influence in their organizations, either formally or informally. This text will give a leader a real hands-on approach to performance improvement. In this text, **performance improvement** means delivering **better** products and services **faster** and at **lower cost**. Leaders are often frustrated and sometimes intimidated by the complexity of modern-day processes and feel helpless to do anything about it. This book provides leaders with an action plan they can implement immediately and not have to wait for Black Belts or Green Belts to do "their thing."

Our intent is to provide the philosophy, strategy, and methodology needed for unleashing the power of performance improvement. It is not our purpose to present an alternative approach to Deming, Juran, or Ishikawa. Instead, we build upon a common, underlying theme that is clearly present in their work. That theme is knowledge. Deming even used the term "profound knowledge" in his teaching and writing. While the philosophies of these and other quality gurus typically have emphasized the "what" of process improvement, this text focuses on the "how" and "why." Knowledge about our processes, products, people, and organization is shown to be the DNA of performance improvement. How we get the right kinds of knowledge requires asking the right kinds of questions. We provide leaders with questions they can use to focus on the proper knowledge base: "Questions Leaders Must Answer" and "Questions Leaders Must Ask." Of course, questions without the correct answers yield little knowledge. Thus, we have also provided the methods needed to properly answer the questions.

This book is not only about learning how to gain knowledge about our processes, products, people, and organization, it's also about **why** we need to do so. It's about delivering value to our customers, enhancing both the bottom and top lines of our businesses, building our intellectual capital, and moving our culture toward a state of structured innovation. It's about return on investment and why some organizations succeed in their performance improvement efforts and others do not. It's about giving leaders something concrete they can use now to drive a performance-enhancing culture. In this light, we show that knowledge has been a key ingredient to any performance improvement initiative in those companies that have successfully implemented the likes of Lean Six Sigma, Design for Six Sigma, Operational Excellence, etc., no matter what the initiative may be called. We present a knowledge based strategy from which the knowledge producing questions can repeatedly make a positive impact on a company's performance.

Most readers should be able to digest the entire text in a 2-hour period, e.g., on a flight between Chicago and Denver. Technical knowledge is not needed to read this text, because where a technical definition is provided, it is given in graphical format to make it easy to understand. The text is written in such a way that each chapter can be read independently from the others and still provide the thrust of the theme for that particular chapter. For example, if one wanted to read about Lean Six Sigma, reading Chapter 5 alone will provide a very good overview of that knowledge generating strategy and methodology. However, if the reader is interested in the historical evolution of performance improvement and how the continuing theme of knowledge generation becomes more powerful using the more modern approaches, reading the chapters in the order they are presented is recommended. This will allow the reader to follow the historical trends and see, for example, why Design for Six Sigma (Chapter 6) has been a natural evolutionary step beyond Lean Six Sigma (Chapter 5).

This edition is considerably different from the original. Because the need for change and its management occur at different levels of granularity, from a Lean Six Sigma project to organizational cultural change, we have devoted an entire chapter, Chapter 2, to understanding and motivating the need for change. Chapter 3 traces some of the original quality gurus' philosophies to a more modern knowledge based philosophy and provides an in-depth discussion of the "Questions Leaders Must Answer." Chapter 4 provides the critical link to knowledge and introduces the concept of a knowledge generating strategy. The "Questions Leaders Must Ask" are addressed in this chapter, and we show how Six Sigma's Define, Measure, Analyze, Improve, and Control (DMAIC) methodology incorporates these questions into a knowledge generating strategy.

We devote entire chapters, Chapters 5 and 6, to Lean Six Sigma and Design for Six Sigma, respectively, because they represent the best knowledge generating strategies available today. The final chapter, Chapter 7, takes knowledge generation to a higher level of abstraction, namely the corporate and enterprise level. In this chapter we introduce a competitive excellence model which incorporates everything that has been developed in the first six chapters into a strategy for preserving and evolving the enterprise. It is at this level that the infrastructure for deploying and implementing knowledge generating strategies such as Lean Six Sigma and Design for Six Sigma becomes the most meaningful. Chapter 7 also shows why a systematic and simple approach to innovation is necessary for the sustained economic viability of any enterprise.

Our experience indicates that a major barrier for success in most organizations is the lack of knowledge about their processes, products, people, and organization. Without adequate knowledge it is difficult to communicate and to make good decisions. Without the right kinds of knowledge, we develop a culture of diverse opinions!! We know that if we can help leaders close this knowledge gap, we will have provided a valuable service. The last thing we want to do is complicate the life of a leader. Therefore, we have made every effort to provide you with something extremely simple, yet powerful, with enough common sense and practicality that you can apply immediately to make performance improvement a daily reality in your organization. After you have read and digested this text, you will agree with what Will Rogers once said: "it's what you know that ain't so that can kill you."

Mark J. Kiemele   Richard C. Murrow   Lee R. Pollock

May, 2007

Acknowledgments

Winston Churchill once said, "Writing a book is an adventure. To begin with, it is a toy and an amusement. Then it becomes a mistress, then it becomes a master, then it becomes a tyrant. The last phase is that just as you are about to be reconciled to your servitude, you kill the monster and fling him about to the public."

The authors wish to thank our families, friends, and colleagues for their part in "slaying the monster." Without them, we would have been "devoured." Each supported us in a unique and valuable way. Our colleagues who are on the road spreading the word of a knowledge based approach to performance improvement deserve immense credit for the popularity of the first edition and the demand for this one. The Air Academy staff has persevered through it all. Mary Bowen, Suellen Hill, Debbi Radke, Denise Rucker, Corky Stevens, and Douglas Vaughn endured the daily pressures of working with us and the multi-tasking required of a team that was dedicated to producing this product while responsible for many other duties as well. Without the outstanding work of Douglas Vaughn, our technical layout and graphics specialist, and Suellen Hill, who provided continuous editing and production support, this edition would not have gone to print.

Very special thanks go to Sue Darby, President of Six Sigma Products Group and our chief editor and publisher, for her continued support and motivation to get this done. We are also extremely grateful to Dr. Steve Schmidt, whose original ideas for providing an underlying philosophy for performance improvement are imbedded in this text.

Finally, we wish to thank all of our clients who valued the original edition and created the pull for this new edition. Without clients and readers, this book would not be needed.

Chapter 1

INTRODUCTION TO KNOWLEDGE BASED MANAGEMENT

"Knowledge has become the key economic resource and the dominant, if not the only, source of comparative advantage."

Peter Drucker

For the last couple of decades, industry has been bombarded with a plethora of improvement initiatives, many of which make bold claims with regard to improvement in customer satisfaction, profit margins, and revenue gains. While some have gained or are gaining more universal acceptance and have shown documented improvements, all have had their successes and failures. Thus, it is not surprising to find many of today's leaders puzzled and perhaps skeptical, wondering "What is next?" Commonly heard statements such as "This is just the next flavor of the month" and "This is just another consultant's ploy" provide evidence to the frustration felt at every level of an organization. Notwithstanding America's penchant for a "new label" for improvement strategies every so-many years and the compounding factor of Sarbanes-Oxley, the scenario is complicated.

For some, the performance improvement puzzle shown in Figure 1.1 can be daunting. Wanting to avoid any further frustration and complexity, the authors of this text are not attempting to contribute a new piece to the puzzle. Rather, our intent is to show the reader and practitioner how all the pieces in the puzzle–and all the "future pieces" of the puzzle–can be tied together into a successful system of business thinking called Knowledge Based Management (KBM). We intend to show that the KBM thought process will accommodate the evolution of societal needs along with the discovery of new methods and techniques to form a systematic approach to enhancing business performance.

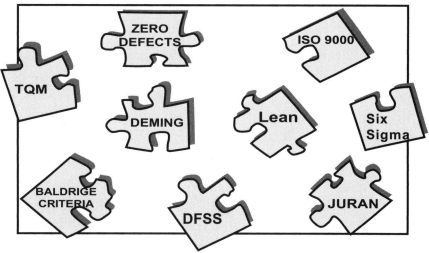

Figure 1.1 The Performance Improvement Puzzle:
"A Set of Disjointed Pieces?" or "Do the Pieces Fit Together?"

At this early point in the text, let us simply define Knowledge Based Management as a systematic approach to enhancing business performance by improving the following:

1) Customer Value

2) Intellectual Capital

3) Top Line (Revenue) Growth

4) Bottom Line (Profit) Growth

5) Cultural Change

Using these five areas as targets for improvement, we can begin to describe a Knowledge Based Management system pictorially as shown in the Input-Process-Output (IPO) diagram in Figure 1.2. An IPO diagram is a visual mechanism to illustrate the key outputs or responses from a process (see the arrows on the right exiting the box). The IPO diagram also shows the key input factors or entities that may influence or impact the outputs. These inputs are shown via the arrows on the left that are pointing to the box.

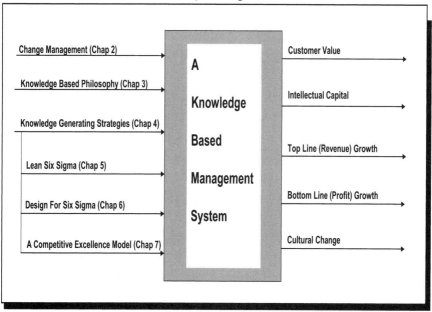

Figure 1.2 Pictorial Representation of A Knowledge Based
Management System

The goal of this text is to carefully investigate the critical inputs for a successful KBM system or process. These inputs will unlock the secrets of success at leading companies such as General Electric, Sony, GlaxoSmithKline, Toyota, Xerox, and many others. At this point, you might be thinking, "Good for these companies that have been successful in their performance improvement efforts, but how would I know if a Knowledge Based Management approach is right for me and my organization?" To help us deal with this issue, consider the following questions:

> **Where are we?**
>
> **Do we need to change?**
>
> **If so, where are we going?**
>
> **How will we get there?**

We will address these questions throughout the text and provide a common sense approach that leads to success. However, it will be necessary to answer these questions in sufficient detail if we are to acquire the knowledge necessary to produce return on investment from our performance improvement efforts.

Webster's dictionary defines **knowledge** as: *familiarity, awareness, or understanding gained through experience or study*. In order to evaluate our knowledge base, we will address two sets of detailed questions. First, to evaluate our knowledge of the management philosophies that lead to industrial competitiveness and success, we will present a list of **Questions Leaders Need to Answer**. Then, to provide an impetus or "pull system" for our knowledge generating capability, we will present a list of **Questions Leaders Need to Ask**. These questions, plus the methods and techniques and deployment approach needed to answer these critical questions, are the key ingredients for a **Knowledge Based Management** system. See Figure 1.3.

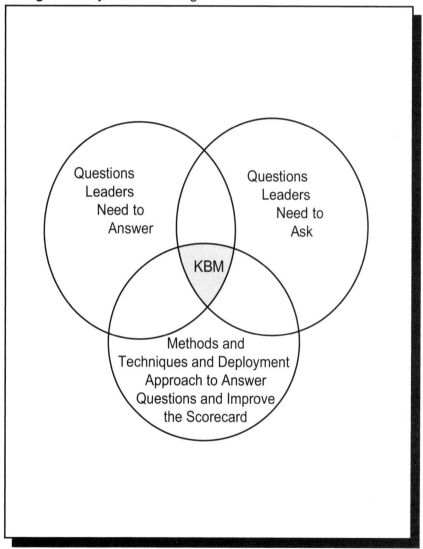

Figure 1.3 Key Ingredients for Knowledge Based Management (KBM)

Good decisions, based more on knowledge than opinion, must be supported with facts and data. Obtaining knowledge from facts and data will require the use of statistics. The need for good statistical reasoning is more important now than ever, as more data will be collected and disseminated in the Colorado Springs area alone in a week than was generated worldwide during the entire 17th century. In other words, statistical thinking will not only be required for performance improvement but for informed citizenship as well. Unfortunately, statistics is often taught as an "end" rather than a simple "means" to the real end which is **knowledge**.

Many non-statistically oriented practitioners want to be able to gain knowledge quickly without being overwhelmed by statistical complexity. There are also those who dislike or distrust statistics because of how it has traditionally been taught or because they believe the well-circulated notion that "you can torture data to make it say anything." Over the last two decades, Air Academy Associates (AAA) has gained a reputation for revolutionizing the communication of statistics. Our "Keep It Simple Statistically (KISS)" approach has gained international appeal because it produces large gains in knowledge from relatively low levels of statistical complexity. See Figure 1.4. The reader should not interpret KISS as being less powerful than a traditional approach to statistics. On the contrary, the KISS approach is even more powerful because it can leverage a whole organization, not just a select few, to be able to act on facts and data. This has been a very important part of the success of our Six Sigma methodology with a host of clients, from manufacturing to transactional and service applications.

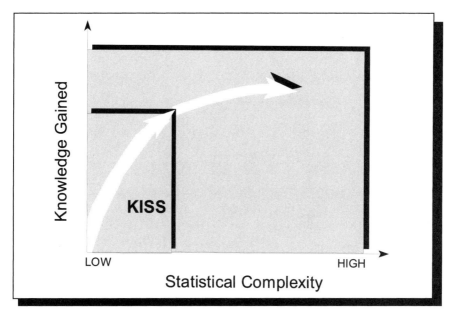

Figure 1.4 Why Advocate a KISS approach?

Statistical practitioners who insist on complicating every improvement opportunity often confuse their customers and stakeholders (managers, scientists, engineers, technicians, etc.) and usually end up in one of the following situations: i) out of a job; ii) constantly battling with their customers and stakeholders; or iii) isolated as an analyst who simply sits in a corner crunching data and is out of the main stream of generating improved performance of products and services.

An apparent advocate of our KISS philosophy is Mr. Craig Barrett, CEO of Intel. In his keynote address to an Accreditation Board for Engineering and Technology (ABET) conference, Mr. Barrett made the following statements:

- **"Statistical literacy is the key to our industrial competitiveness."**

- **"Instructors of statistics courses don't teach Applied Statistics."**

- **"Instructors of engineering courses don't teach Statistics."**

- **"Engineering professors are not statistically literate."**

- **"The customer (industry) is NOT HAPPY."**

The conference was attended by many well-known Deans of Engineering, engineers, and statisticians. We at Air Academy Associates were also represented at that conference and have responded to Mr. Barrett's challenging remarks with three KISS-oriented textbooks: *Basic Statistics: Tools for Continuous Improvement; Understanding Industrial Designed Experiments; and Lean Six Sigma: A Tools Guide*. To many, these texts take a radically new and refreshing approach to presenting powerful statistical techniques in a very digestible manner, as the following quotes indicate:

"This is perhaps one of the most applicable and timely resources for engineers and managers..."

"The designs and methods are presented in a way that facilitates understanding and encourages the use of statistical techniques..."

"The format is ideal for managers and engineers."

"The text is easy to read, emphasizes applications, and contains material not usually found in introductory stats books..."

"The book has done a remarkably good job at reaching its intended audience of college level students taking their first course in statistics, as well as experienced managers and engineers..."

"Kudos to the authors for customer focus, something few authors ever consider beyond their own environment..."

The ultimate compliment on our texts and materials was for Sony to translate them into Japanese for internal use in their company. Lest the reader be swayed that all comments have been positive, here are some "negative" comments:

> *"This is a strange book ... Statisticians will not find this book useful..."*
>
> *"The absence of theory is a glaring weakness. The beauty of statistics is in its derivations and foundations, not in its use to 'get results'... there is too much emphasis on 'getting results'..."*

Although these "negative" comments have been made about our philosophy and KISS approach, the positives far outweigh the negatives; and the number of universities, companies, and organizations adopting our materials and/or services is growing rapidly. Our customers like the KISS approach with a heavy emphasis on using statistics as a means to gaining knowledge.

This approach to reducing statistical complexity has also carried over to another version of KISS: Keep It Simple Software, which we have been developing over the last 19 years. The combined KISS effort has revolutionized how we merge training, statistics, and software to easily obtain the knowledge to solve large industrial problems. Combining the philosophies of Keep It Simple Statistically and Keep It Simple Software has allowed many more people (including those not well versed in statistics or the use of software) to gain knowledge and to improve performance of their products and services by making them better, faster, and at lower cost. We are finding this effect to be even more pronounced in the transactional and service applications than in manufacturing.

Like KISS, there are numerous ideas that we present in this text. These ideas are not academic in nature but stem from the successes we have had while training and coaching more than 80,000 practitioners worldwide. It is our intent that the text be used as a common sense guide for leaders, managers, engineers, scientists, technicians, and analysts as they lead their organizations to competitive excellence and "World Class" status.

Chapter 2

UNDERSTANDING AND MOTIVATING THE NEED FOR CHANGE

"Early on, when culture and change compete, culture wins."

Tom Quan, GlaxoSmithKline

It has been said that "culture eats change for breakfast." Change is tough, because there are always ramifications from change. Our daily lives are impacted by decisions. Do I purchase a new cell phone? Do we change vehicles? Do we move to another neighborhood? Do we change jobs? Change occurs at different levels of abstraction and different levels of magnitude, and the decision "to change or not to change" will have an impact. This is a key point stressed throughout this text. This chapter addresses the management of change and is the first major factor of those we address that will influence a Knowledge Based Management system. See Figure 2.1. We will consider both the performance and technically based aspects of change as well as the human side of change, since all will be key players in any kind of change initiative.

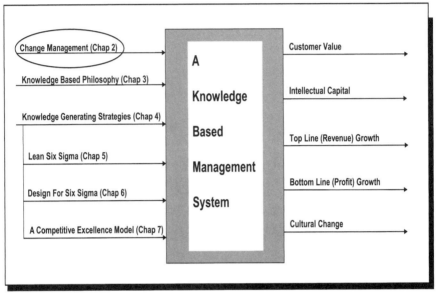

Figure 2.1 KBM IPO Diagram

The need for a disciplined, repeatable improvement strategy is not a fad forced upon us by our customers or a necessary evil imposed by some regulatory agency. Greater product and service value is being demanded by customers and society in general, and if they cannot get that value from a particular provider, they will get it elsewhere. Customers are more knowledgeable and demanding than ever before, and that trend is not going to stop. If we are to move forward, there needs to be sufficient emphasis on improved products, services, and processes. Today's economic mantra is "better, faster, lower cost," and customer value is a function of all of those factors, not just one of them. Many companies today refer to this as quality, cost, and delivery. Nonetheless, inherent in the comparative words of **better**, **faster**, and **lower** is change. Better than what? Faster than what? Lower than what? In fact, it is metrics (or things to measure) from these three categories (better, faster and lower cost) that we will need to get a handle on in order to answer the questions **"Where are we?"** and **"Do we need to change?"**

"Better" metrics include defect rate, error rate, defects per unit, errors per transaction, accident rates (i.e., safety measures), number and kind of customer complaints per time period, etc. Anything having to do with the quality, goodness, or accuracy of a product, service, or transaction would fall in this category. In fact, some companies refer to these quality related performance measures as "Critical to Quality" measures or CTQs. "Faster" metrics are typically linked to time and include things like turn-around-time, cycle time, delivery time, time between bad events, etc. Clearly, the project area or application being studied will be needed in order to make the metric complete, e.g., "cycle time of what," etc. "Cost" metrics are obviously linked to monetary measures such as overhead costs, raw material costs, inventory costs, rework costs, etc. Throughout this text, we will refer to all metrics or performance measures, no matter if they are in the better, faster, or lower cost categories, as Critical to Customer performance measures, or CTCs. The critical characteristic of any CTC is that it must be **measurable**. If something is not measurable, it cannot be a CTC. This is a key concept that will be referred to often later in the text when we refer to Lean Six Sigma projects, as projects target CTCs for improvement. It is through the comparison of these CTCs with our goals, our competition, and our customer needs that we can begin to answer the questions **"Where are we?"** and **"Do we need to change?"**

Interestingly, many leaders in an organization are often opposed to initiating improvement efforts because of the estimated "cost of doing something" to make that change happen. And this cost is a legitimate concern. However, what is often lost or not discussed is the "cost of doing nothing," which is also a legitimate cost. Sometimes the "cost of doing nothing" is referred to as waste or the "cost of poor quality" (COPQ). Without a good handle on where we are with regard to these kinds of costs, it will be difficult to (1) make a good decision and (2) motivate the change if a change is going to occur as a result of the decision.

In order to give the reader a quick "Rule of Thumb" estimate on COPQ or waste, we have combined the "before" and "after" results of many projects from many different clients to obtain the rough estimates shown in Table 2.1. This data has been validated by the likes of General Electric, Sony, Texas Instruments, GlaxoSmithKline, AlliedSignal/Honeywell, and many others. These COPQ estimates include internal failure costs, external failure costs, appraisal costs, prevention costs, and lost opportunity costs, all of which will be defined in more detail in Chapter 4.

defects per unit (dpu)	First Pass Yield (FPY)	COPQ or Waste in terms of % of Revenue
.31	69%	30-40%
.07	93%	20-30%
.006	99.4%	15-20%
.0002	99.98%	10-15%
.0000034	99.99966%	<<10%

Table 2.1 Rough Estimate Guide for COPQ and Waste.

Using Table 2.1 as a reference point and considering an example of a $100 Million per year company, if most of the processes were at a .07 dpu or 93% FPY (this can be measured via appropriate sampling), then we would estimate the waste at about $20-$30M per year. Therefore, if developing a repeatable, disciplined improvement strategy (as outlined in subsequent chapters) could save at least 20% of that COPQ annually (and that is a very conservative estimate), the savings should be at least $4-6M annually. Although it is always better to measure COPQ directly, the reader should note that very good estimates of COPQ can be obtained indirectly by measuring the capability of key processes and using the correlations established in Table 2.1.

Obviously, if the cost of doing something far exceeded the cost of doing nothing, it would not be wise to press on. However, the problem today is that many organizations are not tracking the right metrics in order to understand or quantify the cost of doing nothing. It is difficult to make a good decision if we are comparing something with nothing.

While COPQ is a major factor in determining the need for change, there are other considerations that might also motivate the need for change. These include:

1) Customer perceptions;

2) Stock price, market share, and profit trends;

3) Studying societal needs and the mood of the market;

4) Forecasting the future if no change is made; and

5) Investigating other leading companies and their strategies.

The downfall for some past improvement efforts has been that there was no plan in place to measure the Return on Investment (ROI) from the change initiative. If we have learned anything over the last decade with regard to improvement strategies, it has been that ROI must be measured. The survivability of any change initiative will depend to a large extent on monetary results. In the US anyway, there is nothing that will stick unless it has something to do with dollars. If an improvement strategy provides a capability to deliver measurably better products and services delivered faster and at lower cost, there will be measurable ROI. A company need not be as large as General Electric to show ROI from its improvement efforts. Consider a few examples from a variety of industries:

• Intermedics' Rai Chowdhary began a 4-month quest for quality improvement on the coating of titanium on a cobalt-chrome substrate. The solution to this problem defied all previous medical product expert opinions and approximately 10 years of research from some of the nation's leading material scientists. His efforts in using KISS techniques generated the knowledge to patent the process and save his company from ditching a product which subsequently has generated $60 million of revenue annually.

• JetStream Airways, a small airline company that prides itself on quality service, on-time arrivals and fair fares, invested nearly $1.5 million to install self-service kiosks in the airports they serve. Unfortunately, the airline did not see the reduction in reliance on check-in agents that they expected, and they received complaints about the kiosks from travelers. Using a Six Sigma team to investigate the source of the problems, they applied the Define, Measure, Analyze, Improve, and Control (DMAIC) performance improvement methodology to identify ways to increase kiosk use and decrease the number of check-in agents needed. As a result, they realized up to $2.8 million in cost savings, all without adversely affecting the traveler experience and thus gaining substantial ROI on their original investment. For a detailed analysis of this successful project, please see the article "Underutilization of Airport Kiosks" by Ilona Kirzhner in *iSixSigma Magazine*, Nov/Dec 2005.

•   The mayor of Ft. Wayne, IN, claims that he won re-election by a wide margin based on the city's use of the Six Sigma improvement methodology. Graham Richard, a Democrat whose first term was determined by a narrow 80-vote margin, is a strong proponent of using the business improvement methodology to remove government bureaucracy. The mayor claims his decisive re-election was a result of his administration's performance improvements in city services and government. These included a 50% reduction in missed trash pickups, a reduction in response time to pothole complaints (from an average of 21 hours to 3 hours), and more than $10 million in savings or cost avoidance. (Source: "Six Sigma and the City" by Elaine Schmidt, *iSixSigma Magazine*, Mar/Apr 2006)

•   Kohlberg and Company, a private equity firm specializing in middle-market investing, uses Lean Six Sigma to first determine whether they should buy a business and then to apply it in its strategy for managing the acquired business. Jim Wiggins, a Kohlberg principal who is Chairman and CEO of Holley Performance Group and Chairman of Stanadyne Corporation, two companies in the Kohlberg portfolio, introduced this performance improvement strategy to Kohlberg for the purpose of identifying waste and cost of poor quality and then eliminating it. He sees waste as an "opportunity" and has utilized Lean Six Sigma to save almost

$6 million in hard savings over the last two years in these two Kohlberg companies alone. Reference *iSixSigma Magazine*, Jul/Aug 2006, for the complete story.

• Software developer IDX Systems Corporation in Burlington, VT, which develops business software for healthcare organizations, started applying Six Sigma in 2002. Thomas Butts, IDX President and COO, was brought in from GE to run the company. He says, "I don't differentiate between software versus other industries or markets; part of running any business, as I see it, is having a way to really analyze situations and data, and having the right data to make decisions. So whether it's manufacturing, or services, or software that we offer, the application of Six Sigma is absolutely important to the way we are going to run a business." It has obviously paid off for IDX because they have reduced installation cycle times by 25%, reduced non-billable case efforts by 20%, and improved defect containment effectiveness by 20%. Efforts like this and others translate into a $10 million hard savings for IDX over their first two years of deployment. For a complete summary of this success story, please see *iSixSigma Magazine*, Mar/Apr 2005.

• Parkview Medical Center in Pueblo, CO, has developed a phenomenal quality improvement culture over the last few years. One success story seems to lead to another. Using KISS techniques to properly categorize clinical pneumonia patients, they have increased yearly revenues by more than $100,000. A spin-off team from the clinical pneumonia team increased the success rate on producing good sputum cultures from a benchmarked 35% to an impressive 95%. Extending the KISS principle to their business practices has allowed them to reduce the accounts receivable process cycle time from 82 days down to 40 days, thereby earning them more than $4 million in interest over a 3½ year period. It seems for Parkview, anyway, that where there's a will, there's a way.

The evidence is clear that an improvement strategy can and will affect the bottom line for those who apply it correctly; and a critical key to correct application is to go after the right kind of knowledge, as this is the foundation for ROI and all the subsequent benefits that are derived from it. See Figure 2.2 (The right kind of knowledge is the subject of Chapters 3 and 4). Oftentimes if the required knowledge is missing, the ROI is fleeting and the improvement effort stalls, leaving an organization very disillusioned about its improvement efforts.

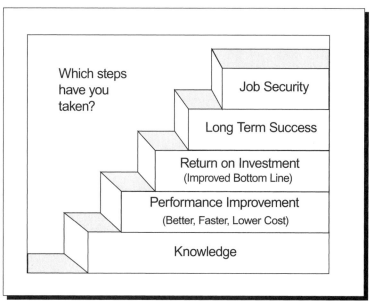

Figure 2.2 Steps Taken to Improve Performance

Besides the performance and technical reasons for change, the human side of change is equally if not more important. Any improvement strategy deployed or implemented will create change in the processes and practices of an organization. Things are the way they are in many organizations because they have always been that way. Many of the processes and practices are based on tradition, and they are imbedded in the culture. Culture produces the soothing effect of comfort, and change disrupts this comfort level. The logical response to change is resistance.

Psychologists Frank and Kelly Petrock of General Systems Consulting Group have a simple model that describes the key ingredients to successful change. Their model states that

$$DD + VF + FS > R,$$

where   DD = Degree of Dissatisfaction in the organization (i.e.,the need),

VF = Vision for the Future (i.e., the vision),

FS = First Steps (i.e., the plan), and

R   = Resistance.

In words, if the combination of need, vision, and plan has more energy behind it than the "resistance to change," then change will take place. It is leadership's responsibility to create sufficient energy to overcome the resistance, and the best way to do so is to take a knowledge based approach to developing the need, vision, and plan. It is also leadership's responsibility to assess the organization's readiness for change and to adopt the means to optimize it. To describe a typical organization's readiness for change, we have developed what we call our Frontier Model, a metaphor that most leaders will recognize. This is shown in Figure 2.3 as a normal distribution segmented into three major areas. The area on the right is occupied by Pioneers. This is clearly a small minority in most organizations; it may not be exactly 10%, but it is most definitely a small percentage. Training alone in an improvement strategy will empower Pioneers, and they will be off and running. Many Six Sigma Black Belts exhibit traits of a Pioneer.

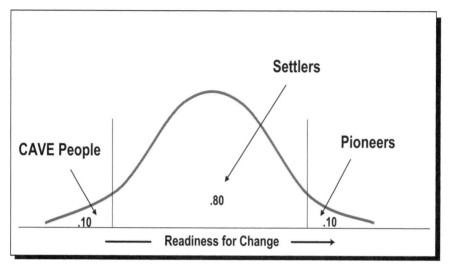

Figure 2.3 Frontier Model

The vast majority of the organization—perhaps not exactly the 80% shown in the middle segment but most certainly a strong majority of the population—will be Settlers. Training alone will NOT empower Settlers. To move the organization forward, leadership must consistently and continually act on this important group. Leadership must set and declare expectations, aligning the reward and recognition system with performance accountability and expectations, in order to motivate these people.

The area on the left, a minority percentage, represents the group called the CAVE (Citizens Against Virtually Everything) People. Nothing will empower these people or motivate them toward change. Make no mistake: these are good people and they come to work every day wanting to do good by doing what they have always done.

Their outlook is one of "we must be doing something good because we are still here and woe be unto those who challenge what we do." It is not always easy to detect CAVE people, but sometimes their dialect, called Cavespeak, can identify them. Table 2.2 provides some typical Cavespeak lines that leadership must understand and know how to combat. The Air Academy approach to CAVE people is to first attempt to move them out of the CAVE with a heavy dose of combined energy from the need, vision, and plan for the change (i.e., improvement strategy)—more on this later. Do not underestimate the amount of energy that will be needed, because it will be more than the leaders of many organizations can muster. Only rarely do we see a phenomenal transformation of a CAVE person becoming a Pioneer. It doesn't happen often, but it is worth the tremendous effort needed to make it happen because the ROI from such a transformation is substantial. Unfortunately, after what might seem to be an overwhelming effort to dislodge people from the CAVE, the CAVE must ultimately be sealed up in order to prevent Settlers from migrating into it. The volatility and expansiveness of the CAVE will be proportional to the level in the organization of its occupants.

- We are already doing that.
- I don't see how this applies to us.
- We need to see success stories from this in our own organization before we could commit.
- It won't work in our culture.

(Continued on next page)

Table 2.2 Cavespeak

- It is too much of a change.
- You're right, but we are different.
- The time is not right for us.
- This is just another flavor of the month.
- Let's form a committee to study this further.
- No organization exactly like ours has ever done this.
- Why do we need this? We are doing fine as is.
- It's too much work. We don't have the people.
- Has any other organization like ours ever done this?
- It may work there, but it won't work here.
- Our people will not be able to handle this change.
- Once we get over_____, we should revisit this.
- This is all good stuff, but _____.
- I can see where this applies to that part of the organization, but not to ours.
- We will have a hard time getting the union to buy into this.
- If we bring this on, our people will rebel – they are already up to their eyeballs in work.
- We are already as lean as can be.
- We don't have anybody else who can work on this.
- If we hold out long enough, this too shall pass.

Table 2.2 Cavespeak

Knowledge Based Management is getting the desired results through changing, adapting, and modifying the existing processes and procedures of both people and organizations. Since changes are accomplished by people, if people are not motivated to change, change will not occur. From our experience, the human side of the change process can be more complicated and confusing than the technical side of change. Hence, knowledge of how people react and cope with change is critical to the success of any organization's implementation strategy. The universal human phenomenon of resistance to change must be managed in order to achieve a profitable and long-lasting performance improvement initiative. The purpose of this chapter is not to present an in-depth study of change management. Rather, we will propose that the following questions be considered by those who are serious about generating positive change.

1.   What are the normal reactions to change?

Psychologists suggest that during a major change in an individual's life certain trends in human behavior take place. This pattern is depicted in Figure 2.4 which illustrates the natural and normal behavior of individuals progressing through the change process. The transition curve depicted in this figure is adapted from Elisabeth Kübler-Ross's *On Death and Dying.*   Kübler-Ross claimed that her "grief cycle" applied not only to the terminally ill but also to anyone who experiences a perceived negative impact from change in one's life.

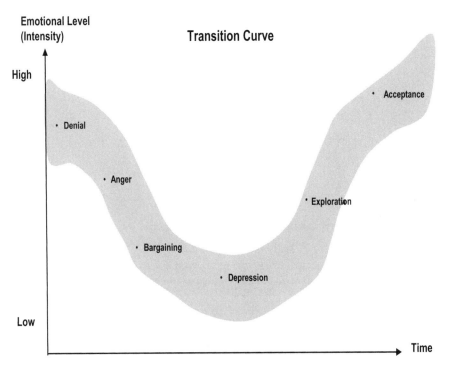

Figure 2.4 Levels of Emotional Intensity During Transition Period

As shown, there are a number of different phases or stages that an individual will go through as change takes place. These different phases can usually be identified by listening to comments that people make. For example,

1. Denial - "This can't be happening." or "I don't believe this."

2. Anger - "I don't want to, I don't have to, and you can't make me."

3. Bargaining - "Maybe we can work something out."

4. Depression - "I don't feel good. I can't deal with this right now."

5.   Exploration - "How about if we try this _____."

6.   Acceptance - "Thanks, I really needed that."

Note from the transition curve, there is not a distinctive separation between phases and each phase has a range of emotional intensity. Consider for example, the case of traumatic loss. The stages and levels of emotional intensity vary from an initial stage of denial to the final stage of acceptance, with steps such as anger, bargaining, depression, and exploration sandwiched between denial and acceptance. The transition curve shown can be used as a roadmap. This roadmap can help us understand what we and others go through when dealing with a major change, even though it may not be a traumatic change. In a less traumatic change, an individual may minimize certain steps or move through the various phases quickly - moving through anger in a short period of time and virtually skipping bargaining and depression. Regardless, an individual needs some time to change as they progress through these natural phases. The amount of time required to change will vary depending on the individual and how they are managed. In other words, if we understand where an individual is in the change process we can modify how we interface with them to help speed up the process.

2.   Why do people resist change?

A variety of reasons exist for people who resist change in the workplace. Some people resist change due to their large investment of time and effort in the "status quo." For example, people who have worked hard for many years to obtain a powerful position could have the most to lose both financially and emotionally. Hence, they have the strongest motivation to maintain the "status quo." If they perceive change as something that decreases their importance or status, they will likely oppose it overtly or covertly.

Another reason to resist change is the "fear of the unknown." This fear is caused by the omnipresent human desire for predictability and sense of control over one's life. Leaving the known for something new is inherently unsettling and involves facing many uncertainties and risks. Fear of any type is a very powerful force and is difficult to overcome.

Tradition and "nostalgia" may also arouse strong emotions, such as: resistance to changing something that is tied to past successes, changing things that have major emotional importance, or abandoning original and long-standing organizational core concepts. From a broader perspective, major resistance is often linked to the pleasant memories of the past and an unwillingness to give them up.

Another reason to resist change might simply be described as pride. Suppose someone interprets the need for change to imply that they failed in the past. In this case, it is very possible for pride to override logical thinking, and resistance to change sets in. From a slightly different angle, a person can resist change if they despise who or what the change represents. For example, if a person has become nauseated with years of listening to "quality this" and "quality that" they may get their hair up every time they associate the need for change with the term "quality."

Finally, the resistance to change may be tied to how it is presented. As someone once said, "No one cares how much you know until they know how much you care." When change is suggested by a person perceived as non-caring or by one who has a self-serving agenda, many people will simply resist.

3. Why do some people openly embrace change?

There exists another group of individuals in an organization that is usually in favor of changes and improvements. Reasons for welcoming change are as diverse as those for resisting change. Some individuals may see a proposed change as a potential for advancement, a chance for new learning, or an avenue for new growth. In other cases, individuals are influenced through team spirit, peer pressure or by strong organization pressures. Individuals who have been very discontent with the "status quo" may see the change as an opportunity for a better future because of their concern over such issues as the downsizing of the business or a lack of personal fulfillment.

There are also people who have a reputation for being the first to try new things. These people might be characterized as having a "pioneering" spirit and can be counted on to readily accept new ideas.

4. Is change always necessary?

No! If everything is in a constant state of change we border on chaos. Change only for the sake of change must be avoided. Furthermore, individuals and organizations need times of stability to evaluate where they are. That is difficult to do if we're always changing.

> **"We trained hard. But it seemed that every time we were beginning to form up we would be reorganized. ...I was to learn later in life that we tend to meet any new situation by reorganizing, and a wonderful method it can be for creating the illusion of progress while producing confusion, inefficiency and demoralization."**
>
> *Petronius Arbiter, 210 B.C.*

On the flip side, improving performance is something we should always be striving for and as such, change should always continue to take place over the long term. It is important, therefore, to discern when stability is needed versus when to push for positive change. This issue is developed further in questions 5 and 6.

5.   What are the key ingredients for successful change?

In order to see successful change take place we will need some measure of the following three ingredients:

a)   a *need* for change

b)   a *vision* for what the change will do for the individual and the organization

c)   a *plan* to make change take place

6.   How do we manage the three ingredients in question 5?

Regardless of our natural response to change or our resistance/willingness to change, unless we clearly see the need for change, it is illogical to pursue it. To develop the need for change, suppose we ask the following question, "What is the cost of doing nothing?" The answer to this question may be difficult to obtain. However, if we do not thoroughly address this question early on, the change process will be painful and may be impossible. Ideally, we should have a task force of key individuals in our organization to explore this question. Motorola did something similar in the late 70's and early 80's. By benchmarking off the Japanese, Motorola saw that their competition had much lower defect rates and cycle times than theirs. The Japanese used these metrics to estimate waste (or Cost of Poor Quality) in their organizations while Motorola (at that time) did not. This benchmarking exercise provided the facts and data which enabled the senior executive to develop strong convictions for change, i.e., the cost of doing nothing was estimated to be very large in terms of dollars.

It is not enough for only senior leadership and management to understand the need for change. Employees must have access to information about their organization that will enable them to also see the need for change. Thus, we must train employees to act like business people and not just hired hands.

> **"If a worker lacks information, he will lack both incentive and means to improve a business."**
>
> *Peter Drucker*

After seeing a need for change, the next step is to visualize what we want to look like when the change is complete. This step requires the need to set measurable stretch goals. Small change is difficult to differentiate from no change at all, whereas stretch goals produce the possibility for substantial improvement. Again for organizations such as Xerox, Motorola, General Electric, Samsung and others, these goals are focused on metrics such as defect rates, cycle times, cost of poor quality and other measurable levels of customer satisfaction.

> **"People seldom hit what they do not aim at."**
>
> *Henry David Thoreau*

Once we establish what we want to look like when the change is complete, the only missing ingredient is the plan to make the change take place. Here is where the heart of KBM fits in. Any plan for successful change that does not address increased knowledge of products, services, processes, people, suppliers and customers is destined to produce poor results. We suggest a careful study of the

Questions Leaders Need to Answer and Questions Leaders Need to Ask. These two sets of questions are presented and discussed in the next two chapters, respectively.

> ## "Without questions, there is no learning."
> *W. Edwards Deming*

Successful change requires that we make every effort to define, evaluate, and communicate the *need, vision* and *plan.* If we are not making every effort to change, we had better go back to the *need* because we obviously do not understand the "cost of not changing, i.e., the cost of doing nothing." As a final note, be aware that frustration levels will get really high when we continue to push *vision* and *plan* on those who do not see the *need.*

7.   How can successful change be sustained?

The most difficult part of change is getting started; however, another challenge is sustaining a positive change. It is our belief that if the need, vision and plan are clearly communicated, most people will want to change. For those who still need a little encouragement, the best tools are the scorecard and the reward system. Most people love to win at what they attempt in life. Those who are ambivalent to winning will still want to be rewarded for what they do. Maintaining change can be as simple as keeping the right score, posting it, and tying it to the reward system.

> ## "If there is no reward,
> ## why does anybody give a damn?"
> *Roger McDivitt*

To summarize this chapter, we conclude with some of the major reasons a change effort may fail. Please reference John Kotter's classic book, **Leading Change,** for more detail.

- Underestimating the sense of urgency for change

- Failing to create a sufficiently powerful core of committed change agents

- Underestimating the power of vision

- Undercommunicating the vision

- Permitting obstacles to block the new vision

- Failing to achieve quick successes

- Declaring victory too soon

- Failing to anchor change firmly into the culture

Table 2.3 Reasons for Change Effort Failing

(Ref. John Kotter, **Leading Change**)

Chapter 3

PHILOSOPHIES FOR GETTING STARTED

"Deming and I didn't create quality in Japan; all we did was give the Japanese a jump start, a push in the right direction."

J.M. Juran

Most of the improvement strategies publicized over the last couple of decades have been based on the philosophies and methods of a select few "quality gurus." Certainly no one can argue with the success of the likes of W. Edwards Deming, J. M. Juran, and K. Ishikawa, who have guided many companies into the quality revolution and on to greater profitability. We firmly believe that regardless of the combination of methods used, the goal for any company should be increased competitiveness (and thus greater chance for survival) through performance improvement of products, services, and associated processes. But how is this achieved? A common but unwritten theme that permeates most of the gurus' philosophies is that enhanced process and product/service knowledge leads to improved performance. But it is the strategy for acquiring that knowledge base that is missing from many companies' performance improvement endeavors. Which guru do we follow? Just as Tiger Woods would not compete in a championship tournament with just a putter, an iron, or a wood, we, like Tiger, recommend a full bag of clubs (methods & tools) that represents the "best of the best" philosophies, tools and techniques. See Figure 3.1.

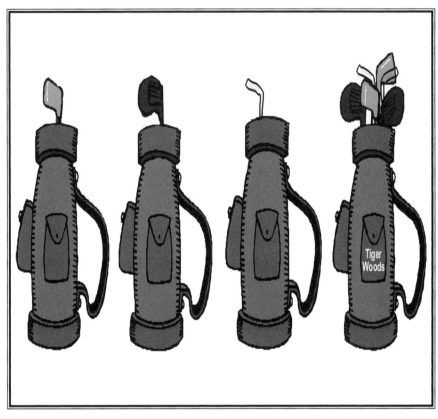

Figure 3.1 Tiger Woods' Bag: A Full Set

In this chapter, we briefly look at some of the ideas from Deming, Juran, and Ishikawa that have launched the performance improvement revolution to its current state. In addition, we develop a knowledge based philosophy that can provide the framework for all of your improvement efforts. See Figure 3.2. To help you properly manage performance improvement from a "knowledge" standpoint, we will discuss in detail a list of **Questions Leaders Need to Answer**. The success of a KBM approach will depend on satisfactorily answering these questions.

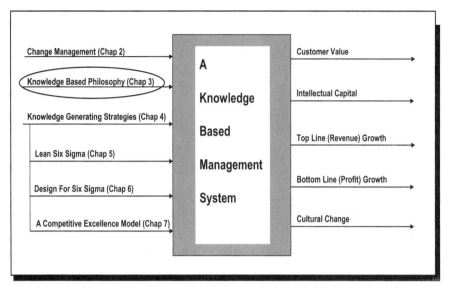

Figure 3.2   KBM IPO Diagram

The previously mentioned quality gurus would agree that the primary responsibility for performance improvement rests with leadership.   Leadership sets the goals and cultural climate of the company, its objectives, and its expectations.   Leadership controls the organization's processes, structure, direction, behavioral reward system, values, vision, policies, materials and human resources.   If leadership has not bought into the idea, and if they don't really see the benefits of enhancing performance, improvement activities will oftentimes lead to exercises in frustration and large wastes of time and money. To quote the National Football League (NFL) coaching legend, Sid Gillman,

> *"Quality Control is <u>only</u> as good as your quarterback. If he goes down, you can take your Quality Control and shove it!"*
>
> Sid Gillman

Quarterbacks are the leaders. They call the plays. A review of NFL history clearly indicates that a team will be hard pressed to get to the Super Bowl without an outstanding quarterback. Just as the big play maker on most Super Bowl teams is the quarterback, big plays in industry rest on leadership's play-calling. Therefore, if a company is going to make a performance improvement sweep around the competition, leadership must make and execute the call.

Before presenting the list of questions leaders need to be able to answer, let's quickly review the philosophies of Deming, Juran, and Ishikawa.

The Deming Philosophy

W. Edwards Deming (1900-1993), physicist, statistician, composer, and world-renowned quality guru, quickly realized that statistical tools without the management structure to implement the tools would realize little, if any, return on investment. His management philosophy is captured in Deming's Fourteen Points. These 14 points, which evolved over the years and are based on Deming's experience with both American and Japanese industry, are presented in Table 3.1.

DEMING'S FOURTEEN POINTS

(1)   Create a constancy of purpose toward the improvement of product and service.   Consistently aim to improve the design of your products.   Innovation, money spent on research and education, and maintenance of equipment will pay off in the long run.

(2)   Adopt a new philosophy of rejecting defective products, poor workmanship, and inattentive service.   Defective items are a terrible drain on a company; the total cost to produce and dispose of a defective item exceeds the cost to produce a good one, and defective items do not generate revenues.

(3)   Do not depend on mass inspection because it is usually too late, too costly, and ineffective.   Realize that quality does not come from inspection, but from improvements on the process.

(4)   Do not award business on price tag alone, but consider quality as well.   Price is only a meaningful criterion if it is set in relation to a measure of quality.   The strategy of awarding work to the lowest bidder has the tendency to drive good vendors and good service out of business. Preference should be given to reliable suppliers that use modern methods of statistical quality control to assess the quality of their production.   (Continued on next page)

Table 3.1 Deming's Fourteen Points

(5) Constantly improve the system of production and service. Involve workers in this process, but also use statistical experts who can separate special causes of poor quality from common ones.

(6) Institute modern training methods. Instructions to employees must be clear and precise. Workers should be well trained.

(7) Institute modern methods of supervision. Supervision should not be viewed as passive "surveillance," but as active participation aimed at helping the employee make a better product.

(8) Drive out fear. Great economic loss is usually associated with fear when workers are afraid to ask a question or to take a position. A secure worker will report equipment out of order, will ask for clarifying instructions, and will point to conditions that impair quality and production.

(9) Break down the barriers between functional areas. Teamwork among the different departments is needed.

(10) Eliminate numerical goals for your work force. Eliminate targets and slogans. Setting the goals for other people without providing a plan on how to reach these goals is often counterproductive. It is far better to explain what management is doing to improve the system.

(Continued on next page)

Table 3.1 Deming's Fourteen Points

(11) Eliminate work standards and numerical quotas. Work standards are usually without reference to produced quality. Work standards, piece work, and quotas are manifestations of the inability to understand and provide supervision. Quality must be built in.

(12) Remove barriers that discourage the hourly worker from doing his or her job. Management should listen to hourly workers and try to understand their complaints, comments, and suggestions. Management should treat their workers as important participants in the production process and not as opponents across a bargaining table.

(13) Institute a vigorous program of training and education. Education in simple, but powerful, statistical techniques should be required of all employees. Statistical quality control charts should be made routinely and they should be displayed in a place where everyone can see them. Such charts document the quality of a process over time. Employees who are aware of the current level of quality are more likely to investigate the reasons for poor quality and find ways of improving the process. Ultimately, such investigations result in better products.

(14) Create a structure in top management that will vigorously advocate these 13 points.

Table 3.1 Deming's Fourteen Points
*Source: Deming, W.E., **Out of the Crisis**,*
MIT Center for Advanced Engineering Study,
Cambridge, MA (1982)

> *"Sound understanding of statistical control is essential to management, engineering, manufacturing, purchase of materials, and service."*
>
> W. Edwards Deming

The Juran Philosophy

Like Deming, Joseph M. Juran spent a good bit of time in Japan during the early 1950's. Juran developed his philosophy and approach over many years, and in 1979, he founded the Juran Institute to provide training and consulting to those wanting to pursue quality improvement. Table 3.2 presents his ten practical steps to quality improvement.

JURAN'S 10 STEPS

(1) Build awareness of the need and opportunity for improvement.

(2) Set goals for improvement.

(3) Organize to reach the goals (have a plan and an organizational structure).

(Continued on next page)

Table 3.2 J. M. Juran's 10 Steps to Quality Improvement

(4)   Provide training.

(5)   Carry out projects to solve problems.

(6)   Report progress.

(7)   Give recognition.

(8)   Communicate results.

(9)   Keep score.

(10)   Maintain momentum by making annual improvement part of the regular systems and process of the organization.

Table 3.2   J. M. Juran's 10 Steps to Quality Improvement
Source: J.M. Juran, **Juran on Planning for Quality***,*
The Free Press, New York (1988)

"Product and service quality requires managerial, technological, and statistical concepts throughout all the major functions in an organization."

J.M. Juran

The Ishikawa Philosophy

Kaoru Ishikawa, a Japanese engineer with noted accomplishments in the quality arena, sees Quality Improvement (he referred to it as Quality Control) as a thought revolution in management. He has developed a list of things that top management must do. We present this list in an abbreviated form.

ISHIKAWA: WHAT MUST TOP MANAGEMENT DO?

- Study quality improvement ahead of anyone else in your company and understand the issues involved.

- Establish the policies towards promoting quality improvement efforts—what the general attitudes will be.

- Specify the priorities for implementing quality improvement and the short and long term goals.

- Assume a leadership role in making quality improvement happen.

- Provide a means for educating the people.

- Check to see if quality improvement is implemented as planned.

(Continued on next page)

Table 3.3 K. Ishikawa's List of Things Top Management Must Do

• Make clear the responsibility of top management.
• Establish a system of cross functional management.
• Drive home the notion that the outputs from your process are inputs to your customers.
• Provide leadership towards making a "breakthrough" happen.

Table 3.3 K. Ishikawa's List of Things Top Management Must Do
Source: K. Ishikawa, **What is Total Quality Control?**,
Prentice Hall, Englewood Cliffs, N.J. (1985)

A Knowledge Based Philosophy

The three previous improvement philosophies have captured a significant following with much success. Yet many leaders see these philosophies as emphasizing the "what" of performance improvement, and they struggle with "how" to make it happen. Knowledge Based Management (KBM) is an extension of the works of Deming, Juran, and Ishikawa with a focus on the "hows."

Deming frequently used the term "profound knowledge." We believe that profound knowledge implies the ability to answer profound questions. Therefore, the guiding principles of KBM are centered around a set of specific Questions Leaders Need to Answer. See Table 3.4. Readers should test themselves on these questions before reading beyond Table 3.4. Correctly answering these questions will lay the ground work for successfully enhancing performance improvement.

QUESTIONS LEADERS NEED TO ANSWER

1. What are your products and services and who are your customers? Do you know the value proposition for each customer?

2. What perceptions do your customers have of your products and services? How do you know? Are you asking your customers the right questions?

3. Do you believe that waste and quality issues are important to your company? Why? Which ones?

4. What is your company's current share of the total market? Can improvement efforts assist you in increasing the market share and/or increasing profits? How?

5. Are you actively pursuing breakthrough as well as continuous improvement in your areas of responsibility that link to customer value? How?

6. How many hours per week have you actually spent over the last three months and how many hours per week do you currently have scheduled on your calendar that are devoted strictly to the removal of waste and variation?

(Continued on next page)

Table 3.4 Questions Leaders Need to Answer

7. How often per week do you solicit feedback from the people you manage? What kind of feedback do you solicit? What do you do with the feedback?

8. What are the right knowledge-generating and improvement-oriented questions leaders need to ask their people? What methods or tools can be used to answer them?

9. Have you deployed and implemented an improvement strategy with a disciplined methodology and toolset and associated infrastructure to predictably generate bottom-line results?

10. Are your people properly trained to successfully use the latest and best improvement methodologies and tools? What is your Return on Investment (ROI) from the training? Do you have a standard procedure for documenting the improvement efforts and results? What is it?

11. What barriers do your people face when trying to improve the way your company does business? What are you doing to remove these barriers?

12. On what measures of performance that relate to these issues are you evaluated? Are you held accountable for these metrics? What are the specific improvement goals for them?

(Continued on next page)

Table 3.4 Questions Leaders Need to Answer

13. How much waste does your company have? That is, what is the company's Cost of Waste or Cost of Poor Quality, both in raw currency amounts and also in percent of revenue? Is it getting better, staying the same, or getting worse? How much of that waste exists or originates in your area of responsibility?

14. Do you have a plan that will, one year from now, show evidence that you made a difference? And what do you predict that evidence will show?

Table 3.4 Questions Leaders Need to Answer

How the leaders and top-level/mid-level managers answer these questions is crucial to the long term success of any company. In the following pages we discuss each question in more depth.

QUESTIONS LEADERS NEED TO ANSWER

1. What are your products and services and who are your customers? Do you know the value proposition for each customer?

Obviously, a leader needs to thoroughly understand what his/her company is all about. Very specific information is required to successfully answer this question. We are often amazed with what we hear when we ask leaders who their number one customer is and what their number one product or service is. Leaders in the same business unit and referring to the same customer sector often give conflicting answers. What does the data say? That should not be a hard question to answer. Mission and vision statements can help us understand our company's purpose and thus help us answer this question.

It seems that any company should know why it is in business and where it is going. In fact, perhaps the best mission statement is "to make a profit." After all, that is why any company, aside from the non-profits, is in business. However, we need to go well beyond that to understand and convey our mission. In writing a mission statement, ask yourself:

1. *What do we produce and/or what service do we provide?*
2. *What characteristics of this product or service make it valuable for our customers?*

In writing a vision statement, ask yourself:

1. *How are we going to ensure that we can compete in the future?*
2. *What things, specifically, do we need to do in order to lead the competition in our industry?*

Mission and vision statements are not meant to be complex expositions, but they should be written in a way that can help drive the company for many years. Specifically, they should:

- *be short and concise,*
- *convey what you are deeply passionate about,*
- *tell what you are the best in the world at or can be the best in the world at, and*
- *communicate, perhaps implicitly, what drives your economic engine.*

Mission and vision statements should inspire, motivate, and provide focus internally. They should also be external facing, conveying to current and future clients what it is you do, with indicators pointing to why and how you do it. The why and how may be implicit, based on the wording, but it should provoke a potential client to ask questions to gain further detail and knowledge. Everything a company does should have some sort of linkage to the mission or vision statements. The goodness of such statements is measured by how well they are communicated to the employees and customers and by the level of commitment from senior leadership. Organizational climate surveys are one means of measuring this communication and commitment.

Example:

Our company, Air Academy Associates, trains and consults in the area of performance improvement and competitive excellence. We specialize in the tools (many of which are statistical in nature) and making them very easy to use at any level of any organization.

In developing our mission statement, we would ask:

1. What do we produce and/or what service do we provide?

Our physical products are textbooks, course notebooks, software, and training aids; and our services are training, coaching, and mentoring of anyone in the organization, from the CEO to the hourly employees. Together, our products and services produce knowledge for our clients to help them improve their competitive position in the marketplace.

2. What characteristics of this product/service make it a valuable commodity to our customers?

Our products are very easy to read, understand, and use; and coupled with the experience, expertise, and passion of our educators and coaches, our approach can leverage the power of the knowledge generating vehicle that we deliver to our clients. The Keep It Simple Statistically (KISS) approach helps create an environment amenable to improvement and innovation. It also provides a capability to anyone who touches our products and services. Furthermore, we have the human resources and advanced problem solving capacity to solve our clients' toughest problems and to transfer this capability to them. All of this is contained in an enterprise-wide plan we provide our clients that will help guide them to a state of competitive excellence and a profitable future.

Our resulting mission statement is as follows:

Our mission is to build intellectual capital for the betterment of business; to preserve the useful, perfect the valuable, and promote a culture of continuous innovation.

Hopefully, the expertise and service we provide our clients, along with the passion, shine through in this statement. Everything we do will be linked in some way to our mission statement. Without a clear understanding of and commitment to our organization's mission and vision, any further efforts will lack direction and alignment.

> ## *"Where there is no vision, the people perish."*
> Prov 29:18

> ## 2. What perceptions do your customers have of your products and services? How do you know? Are you asking your customers the right questions?

Customer surveys and questionnaires, along with focus groups, are some of the more common ways of getting data on customer perceptions. Do we have a systematic approach of collecting this data so that we can quickly detect trends or shifts in perception? If we don't have the data, it will be hard to understand the voice of the customer. Leaders commonly voice their "knowledge" of customers and why the company should move in a certain direction based on that "knowledge." But one has to wonder how much of that "knowledge" is pure conjecture or, at best, based on happenstance. Leaders tend to use the term "data" a lot. But when asked to provide the data, some leaders have a hard time showing that a statement they may have made about customers is nothing more than pure opinion. Oftentimes those opinions are motivated by information politics within a company. Understanding the voice of the customer (VOC) is difficult. A carefully designed process must be used to properly collect VOC data, because the validity of the analysis of that data will depend on how it is collected. Many leaders are not aware that the information content in data is critically dependent on the way the data is collected. A case in point that received national attention was the exit poll data in the 2004 Bush/Kerry presidential election. Why did that data not point in the correct direction? After all, they were exit polls. The answer is simple. The sampling plans for collecting the data were grossly inadequate, and in an election this close, it was easy to draw the wrong conclusion. The good news is there are tools that can help us collect VOC data properly.

A common misperception that must be addressed here is that customer satisfaction can predict customer loyalty. Customer satisfaction surveys that indicate customers are "satisfied" should not be deemed reassuring. Dr. Tom Connellan, President of Performance Research Associates and author of the best-selling **Knock Your Socks Off** *series, has done extensive research in the area of customer satisfaction and customer loyalty. A major finding of his research is contained in what he calls the "Customer Retention Grid." This grid is shown below in Figure 3.3.*

Customer Retention Grid*

OUTCOME		Dissatisfied	Satisfied	Dazzled
	Value Added	At Risk	Loyal	Advocate
	Satisfactory	Searching	At Risk	Loyal
	Fails	Gone	Searching	At Risk

PROCESS

*Copyright Dr. Tom Connellan - Used with permission

Figure 3.3 The Customer Retention Grid

If a customer indicates that his or her experience, outcome-wise, with a product or service is as shown on the vertical axis (3 major categories) and the process of doing business with the provider is as shown on the horizontal axis (also 3 major categories), then the customer status can be described by the word that is shown in each of the 9 boxes. For example, if a customer indicates that the outcome of his experience with the product/service failed and that he was also dissatisfied with the process of dealing with the provider, that customer is "Gone." The word "Searching" indicates that, even though the customer is not gone, he is going, i.e., he is actively searching for alternatives. The main diagonal being all "At Risk" entries is a key point in that even if a customer indicates he is both satisfied with the outcome and satisfied with the process of dealing with the provider (the middle box), the customer, although maybe not actively searching for alternatives, will jump if the appropriate opportunity arises. Loyalty occurs only in the 3 upper right boxes, meaning that we must exceed satisfaction in at least one of the dimensions and maintain at least the status quo in the other. An advocate is a customer who is not only loyal but one who also says good things about you. We have found this model applies to internal customers and stakeholders as well as to external customers. That is, "gone" could very well mean psychologically or emotionally absent, not necessarily physically gone. Being "gone" has huge ramifications for how people work together within organizations. The Customer Retention Grid applies to all companies and businesses, and leaders should use it to help them manage the experience of both their internal and external customers.

> **"If you've higher priorities than meeting your customers' expectations, you're in a whole lot more trouble than any book is going to bail you out of."**
>
> *John Guaspari*

---

3. Do you believe that waste and quality issues are important to your company? Why? Which ones?

---

*The intent of this question is to see if the leader understands the entire spectrum of improvement issues. It will also expose those who simply give performance improvement "lip service." For example, if a manager answers "yes" to part one but cannot explain why or which ones, then he/she doesn't really know what is going on in the organization. Many Six Sigma Champions or Sponsors struggle with identifying potential project areas, an indication that they don't have a handle on this question. Various improvement issues should be discussed. An improvement issue is anything that will enable us to make our product or service **better** and do it **faster** and at **lower cost**. For example, defect rate, yield, variation, cycle time, product/process development time, start-up time, cost of poor quality, waste, price, customer satisfaction, profits, reliability, safety, environmental impact, etc., are some of the more common performance measures targeted for improvement.*

The improvement issues that are important to an organization are the ones that drive the key metrics by which that organization measures success. Our research has shown that companies which direct their improvement efforts toward the business measures on the "balanced scorecard" will achieve greater Return on Investment

(ROI) from their efforts. A balanced scorecard will include metrics related to at least the following: customer, financial, internal business process, supplier and employee.(The discussion of Question 12 later in this chapter will provide further detail on scorecards.)

---

4.   What is your company's current share of the total market?   Can improvement efforts assist you in increasing the market share and/or increasing profits? How?

It is crucial that leaders understand and believe deep down in their hearts that improving performance (if done correctly) will have a substantial impact on the bottom line. It is sad that many companies who currently experience large annual growth don't feel the need to enhance improvement until next year's projection levels out or declines. Whether your company is in a high growth mode or not, improving performance will help optimize the bottom line results. Managers must not only believe this but also be "on fire" rather than "lukewarm" about implementation.   It is unfortunate that many companies do not embrace process and product improvement until they are on their death beds. By then, the seeds of destruction may be too well germinated to reverse the lethal trend. That is why we must continuously target and plan our improvement efforts. Anything less will lead to increased levels of frustration and confusion and possibly failure.

---

5.   Are you actively pursuing breakthrough as well as continuous improvement in your areas of responsibility that link to customer value? How?

If a leader has answered questions 1 through 4 satisfactorily but yet cannot give specific examples of success, the "lips" and the "heart" are not saying the same thing. See Figure 3.4

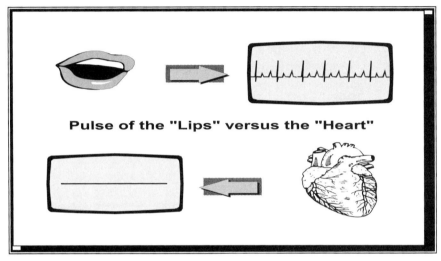

Figure 3.4 Do the Lips Reflect the True Nature of the Heart When it Comes to Commitment to Improved Performance?

*Actively pursuing performance improvement is more than talking about or even initiating an improvement program. It involves leadership participation, support, and commitment, as well as training. (Later in this chapter we suggest **Questions Leaders Need to Ask** which will help you get started on a knowledge generating strategy.)*

> 6. **How many hours per week have you actually spent over the last three months and how many hours per week do you currently have scheduled on your calendar that are devoted strictly to the removal of waste and variation?**

Those who have strong convictions about removing waste and variation will naturally integrate the time into their daily activities. Others may need to have specific time entered in their schedule until it becomes a natural part of how they do business.

> **"If it's not scheduled on the boss's calendar it's not getting done!"**
>
> *Jan Gaudin*

Leaders need to know not only where and with which activities they spend their time but also where the people they supervise spend their time. Pareto charts and Pareto analysis of time spent are valuable tools for process improvement, because Cost Of Poor Quality (COPQ) is usually correlated to those activities with high time utilization. Please reference Figure 3.5 and note the reversal of "Fire Fighting" and "Fire Prevention" in the two Pareto diagrams. Of course, the reward system in an organization has much to do with how one spends his or her time. For example, if the rewards structure emphasizes "fire fighting," the system could unknowingly be generating "arsonists."

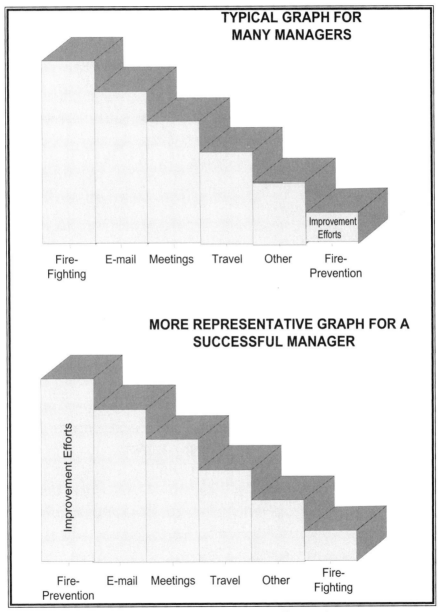

Figure 3.5 Utilizing Time Effectively

> 7. **How often per week do you solicit feedback from the people you manage? What kind of feedback do you solicit? What do you do with the feedback?**

Although leaders have the responsibility for successfully implementing an improvement strategy, the best ideas of how to do it are often in the minds of those who deal with the job details on a daily basis. Enlighten your employees that their job security is directly tied to how competitive the company is, and they will be volunteering to give you feedback on what should be done. Make sure you are ready to listen and willing to implement the good ideas. What is the status of your company's suggestion (or ideas) program? This is a valuable source of information and, if used properly, can be an important motivational factor for employees.

> **"If you overlook information from employees, you overlook probably the most valuable source of customer information you have."**
>
> *Dr. Tom Connellan*

Another important avenue for gaining useful information is to evaluate the climate within the company. A simple list of well thought-out questions can be used to obtain feedback on the attitudes and presumptions of all employees. Employees must always be kept in the loop with regard to the results of an organizational survey and if any action is being taken as a result of the survey. The bottom line is not to let your organizational chart resemble the one shown in Figure 3.6.

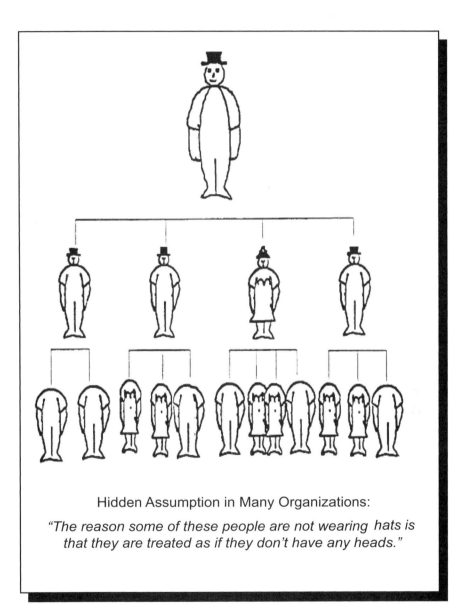

Hidden Assumption in Many Organizations:

"The reason some of these people are not wearing hats is that they are treated as if they don't have any heads."

Figure 3.6 Don't Let Your Organizational Chart Look Like This!

Source: Quality First, Dr. Myron Tribus

> **8.** **What are the right knowledge-generating and improvement-oriented questions leaders need to ask their people? What methods or tools can be used to answer them?**

Our experience indicates that many leaders don't know the right questions to ask. In fact, some leaders are often intimidated by their lack of process knowledge. However, a generic set of questions will empower most leaders to find out the professional knowledge level of their employees. The next set of questions is recommended for managers who want to know what the corporate knowledge level is for a given activity (process, product, or service oriented). Obviously, not every activity will require that all 14 questions be answered.

QUESTIONS LEADERS NEED TO ASK

1. Which value stream are you supporting and who is the recipient of the value, i.e., who is the customer? Who is the value stream owner and who are the players or team members? How well does the team work together?

(Continued on next page)

Table 3.5   Questions Leaders Need to Ask

2. Within the value stream, which process or processes have the highest priority for improvement? Show me the data that led to this conclusion.

For the process or processes targeted for improvement,

3. How is the process performed? How does the value flow? What activity is value added and what is non-value added?

4. What are the process performance measures, i.e., how will we gauge if a process is improving? Why did we choose those? How accurate and precise is the measurement system? Show me the data.

5. What are the customer-driven requirements or specifications for all of the performance measures? Are the process performance measures in control and how capable is the process? Show me the data. What are the improvement goals for the value stream or process performance measures?

6. What kinds of waste and cost of poor quality exist in the value stream or process and what is the financial and/or customer impact? Show me the data.

(Continued on next page)

Table 3.5 Questions Leaders Need to Ask

7. What are all the sources of variability in the value stream or process and which of those do we control? How do we control them and what is our method of documenting and maintaining this control? Show me the data.

8. Are any sources of waste or variability supplier-dependent? If so, what are they, who are the suppliers, and how are we working together to eliminate waste and variability? Show me the data.

9. What are the key input variables that affect the average and standard deviation of the measures of performance? How do you know this? Show me the data.

10. What are the relationships between the measures of performance and the key input variables? Do any of the key input variables interact? How do you know for sure? Show me the data.

11. What settings or values for the key input variables will optimize the measures of performance? How do you know this? Show me the data.

(Continued on next page)

Table 3.5   Questions Leaders Need to Ask

12. For the optimal settings of the key input variables, what kind of variability still exists in the performance measures? How do you know? Show me the data.

13. Have we implemented a process flow and control system to sustain the gains and continuously improve the process? Show me the data.

14. How much improvement has the value stream or process shown in the past six months? How much time and/or money have our efforts saved the company? Show me the data.

Table 3.5   Questions Leaders Need to Ask

> *"If we would have new knowledge, we must get a whole world of new questions."*
>
> *Susan K. Langer*

Knowing the right questions to ask is one thing, but we also need to know the most powerful methods available to get answers. Just as we would not tolerate an engineer using a slide rule for mathematical calculations, or a secretary using an ordinary typewriter to type a letter, we should not allow scientists and engineers and employees in general to use antiquated problem solving techniques. Therefore, it is extremely important that leaders not only know the right questions to ask but also are familiar with the best tools to be used to answer these questions. When a leader sends someone to training there should be an expectation of how that person will utilize the training back on the job.

The next four chapters will expand on each of these questions and provide the best strategies and methods that are available today to answer them. This type of knowledge is a minimum for a leader to successfully implement process improvement in his/her area.

---

9. **Have you deployed and implemented an improvement strategy with a disciplined methodology and toolset and associated infrastructure to predictably generate bottom-line results?**

In order to repeatedly realize the benefits of process improvement activities, there must be some sort of improvement strategy associated with the effort. This is the premise of the scientific method. The strategy must be repeatable, reliable, predictable, and actionable to any process, product, or service. Over the years, many process improvement strategies have emerged. Deming's **Plan-Do-Check-Act (PDCA)** *cycle,* **FOCUS (F***ind a process to improve;* **O***rganize a team that knows the process;* **C***larify current knowledge of the process;* **U***nderstand causes of process variation;* **S***elect the process improvement),* **PCOR (P***rioritize,* **C***haracterize,* **O***ptimize,* **R***ealize) and Six Sigma's* **DMAIC (D***efine,* **M***easure,* **A***nalyze,* **I***mprove and* **C***ontrol) are some of the most notable. It matters less what we call the improvement strategy than the infrastructure in which it is imbedded.*

Figure 3.7 illustrates a Knowledge Based Business Infrastructure showing the processes which are aligned with the improvement strategy. The improvement strategy is represented in this figure by the "Wheel of Fortune," the circular, repeatable improvement strategy, whether it is called PDCA, DMAIC or whatever. What is important to note is that the improvement strategy is surrounded by many activities, including project selection and project results which are cycled back to the business scorecard.

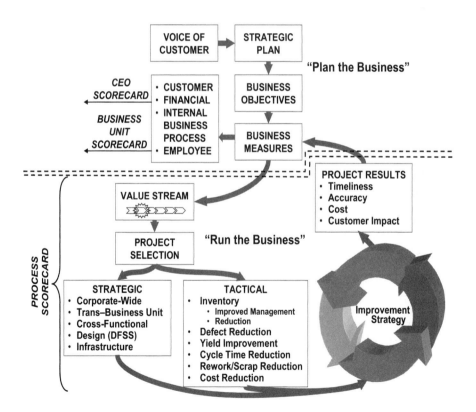

Figure 3.7 Knowledge Based Business Infrastructure

While Figure 3.7 establishes the "process" infrastructure, the "people" infrastructure is equally important. In building a successful infrastructure for an improvement strategy, there are key people who integrate into the process infrastructure. Borrowing from the Six Sigma lexicon, some of these are shown in Figure 3.8.

Figure 3.8 Building the People Infrastructure

Executive leadership is responsible for planning the business and making sure that leadership alignment and sponsorship of the projects are all in place. Champions manage the interfaces between planning the business and running the business. This includes proper project selection so that the projects are aligned with business objectives. Champions are also responsible for making sure the project results impact the business scorecard, as shown in Figure 3.7. Black Belts and Green Belts are those who receive extensive training in the methods and tools of the improvement strategy in order to make the wheel of fortune turn–and turn quickly. They are the project executioners. Much more information concerning this question will be provided in Chapters 5-7 where we discuss in detail the deployment and implementation of some specific knowledge generating improvement strategies like Lean Six Sigma and Design for Six Sigma. Two critical terms that have been used in this discussion of Question 9 are "projects" and "training." These will come to life in our discussion of the next question.

---

10. Are your people properly trained to successfully use the latest and best improvement methodologies and tools? What is your Return on Investment (ROI) from the training? Do you have a standard procedure for documenting the improvement efforts and results? What is it?

---

*The key part of this question is Return on Investment (ROI) from training. Training can be a divisive issue in an organization. When budgets need shrinking, the training budget is the first to be cut in many organizations. However, if we **really know** the relationship between training and ROI, maybe we would have the information needed to make an informed decision. The effectiveness and impact of training has been studied by many people over many years. Professor Donald Kirkpatrick (**Training**, March 1995) developed a model that can be used to evaluate training at 4 different levels which become increasingly more difficult to measure. See Figure 3.9.*

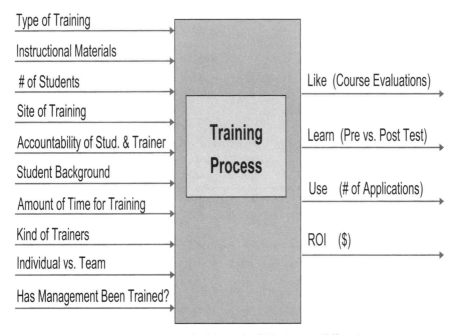

Figure 3.9 Kirkpatrick's Model of Training Effectiveness

*The first level, and the easiest to measure, is to answer the question, "Did the students **like** the training?" While many dismiss this level as trivial and not really telling us if the training was effective, Kirkpatrick found that it is far from meaningless because if a student does not perceive the training to be applicable to the job and easy to digest, it probably won't be. At any rate, this first level is easy to measure and can be accomplished via course surveys. The second level of the Kirkpatrick model addresses the question of "Did the students **learn** the material they were taught?" Although maybe not as easy to measure as the first level, determining if a student learned the material is still relatively easy. Pre and post tests can be administered in a reliable and valid manner to determine the extent of learning. Where the going gets tough, according to*

*Kirkpatrick, is measuring Levels 3 and 4. "Do the (now former) students actually **use** the training in their jobs?" and even more important, "What is the **Return on Investment (ROI)** from our training dollars?" To be able to evaluate training at levels 3 and 4 will require an organizational support structure such as the one shown in Figure 3.7 and a company wide emphasis on performance improvement. The vehicle for measuring the **"use"** of and **"ROI"** from training is the **project**.*

Modern day improvement strategies like Six Sigma require the execution of projects using the Define, Measure, Analyze, Improve, and Control (DMAIC) methodology. Because there is substantial investment in training Six Sigma Black Belts and Green Belts, measuring the ROI from training is a major reason that we do projects. Another reason is the focus that a project brings to an improvement effort. What we know won't work is this: training people in an improvement method and then telling them to go out and do good. What does work is providing the training to execute the DMAIC method, while also providing the infrastructure needed to ensure that successful project execution and measurement of ROI can take place. The deployment and implementation of a Six Sigma DMAIC method is a major difference between more modern day improvement strategies like Six Sigma and those of the past. We will address this difference in later chapters.

It is alarming that most employees in industry are not given a hard copy or electronic notebook containing all of the accumulated knowledge for the processes they are responsible for. That means that any prior knowledge gained was lost when the employee took over the job. In this situation any new employee has to start over gathering knowledge–a very expensive practice. This scenario is exacerbated for companies with high turnover rates. Gaining knowledge is important, but without good documentation and communication we will continually "re-invent the wheel." In today's competitive marketplace, business units–whether they be in government, industry, or academia–do not have this luxury. Resources–people, time, and money–are limited. In order to gain ROI, we will have to do more with less.

Furthermore, many mandated quality improvement efforts such as ISO-9000 (international quality standard), QS-9000 (automotive industry standard), D1-9000 (Boeing supplier standard), Quality Systems Review (QSR, Motorola standard), Process Characterization (electronics industry standard), and Process Validation (FDA regulatory standard for pharmaceuticals and medical devices) are simply a repackaging of what should have already been documented in an activity notebook.

---

11. What barriers do your people face when trying to improve the way your company does business? What are you doing to remove these barriers?

If leaders don't know the barriers their people face, how can they lead their employees to success? One of the primary roles of a Six Sigma Champion is to remove barriers to project completion. Table 3.6 depicts the results of a survey of more than 1000 of our class participants who came from a variety of work environments. The individual responses have been grouped into seven major categories so we can better focus on how to remove those barriers. We suspect these barriers show up to some extent in almost every organization.   How many of these barriers exist in your organization, and what are you doing to remove them?

*Consider the last barrier listed under attitude and motivation: lack the will to win.   If we **lack the will to win**, then losing will be a self-fulfilling prophecy. Also consider this: if we truly have the will to win, nothing short of death will stop us from moving forward.*

**"Not to know is bad;
not to wish to know is worse."**

African Proverb

BARRIERS TO PROCESS IMPROVEMENT

Management	Time	Communication
• Lack of leadership	• Too busy firefighting	• Poor documentation
• Few role models	• People are weary from long hours	• Culture not right for sharing knowledge
• Unclear direction	• Improper time management	• Poor knowledge of customer needs
• Not willing to increase emphasis on gaining complete knowledge in R&D and design	• Duplicated effort	• Don't let suppliers know how to help us
• Not willing or knowledgeable to ask the right questions	• Too many arguments without facts and data	• Inability to properly present something
• Does not encourage enough time to plan	• Perception that new tools take too much time	• Communicate to managers with emotion instead of facts, data and dollars
• Too many layers	• Too many unproductive meetings	• Conflicting messages
• Wants immediate results versus substantial growth in knowledge through use of scientific method	• Timeline pressure	• Information politics
• Don't track the right metrics	• Too busy reorganizing	• Tools for properly communicating process information not known or used
• Ignorant of the new tools for success		
• Not focused on knowledge gained per resource per unit time		
• Continued emphasis on old ways of doing business		
• Reluctant to support new methods		
• Inadequate emphasis on waste (COPQ) identification and reduction		

Table 3.6 Barriers to Process Improvement and Project Completion

AND PROJECT COMPLETION

Training	Resources	Reward System	Attitude and Motivation
• Not enough people properly trained	• Limited resources	• Promotes firefighting	• Laziness
• Inability to think and use common sense	• Insufficient manpower	• Supports traditional power centers	• Don't perceive problems as threatening
• Some people need a refresher course	• Insufficient internal experts to assist others	• People are not held accountable	• Rush to get results without planning
• Management last to be trained versus first	• Inadequate or inappropriate use of outside consultants	• People (groups) compete against each other versus helping	• Easier to blame others than to take responsibility
• Need more motivation in training of basic tools	• Improper allocation of resources	• Perception that powerful tools will uncover poor decisions	• Critical and/or negative attitudes
• Need for a mentor program		• No consequences for not implementing continuous improvement	• Resistance to change
• Need for follow-up assistance			• Professional firefighters feel threatened
• Suppliers need to be trained			• New concepts take time
• Not enough emphasis on COPQ, how to identify it and reduce it			• Fear of failure using new methods
• Unqualified trainers			• Fear of downsizing
• Training is not JIT			• Unwilling to share what you know with others
• Lack of funding			
• Not enough emphasis on ROI			• Lack of the "will to win"

Table 3.6 Barriers to Process Improvement and Project Completion

> ### 12. On what measures of performance that relate to these issues are you evaluated? Are you held accountable for these metrics? What are the specific improvement goals for them?

Metrics are nothing more than specific measures that one can accumulate, teach, and evaluate. The posting of these metrics and how we use them to hold management accountable will, to a large degree, define your company's culture. As a famous coach once said,

> ## "If you are not keeping score, you are just practicing."
> Vince Lombardi

*Thus, keeping score drives the strategy of the game, and careful consideration must be given as to what the **proper** metrics to be posted really should be. For example, in football the scoreboard reflects the number of points scored by each team. Imagine the strategy of the game if, instead of number of points, we posted only the number of first downs! That is, the number of first downs determined whether we won or lost. We could radically change the playing strategy overnight by posting a different scorecard. The long pass, punts and field goals would disappear. The game would be more of a series of four downs for ten yard efforts.*

The same thing is true in industry. If the score only reflects products shipped, services rendered, timelines, and budgets, you will rarely get ROI from process improvement. See Figure 3.10. If you want reductions in COPQ, cycle time, number of changes, number of defects, number of customer complaints, etc., you will need to post it, track it and hold management accountable. Without the proper scorecard, management will keep practicing but will never get into the real game. Use Table 3.7 as a guideline and worksheet to seek out metrics in all vital areas.

Figure 3.10 Example of an Incomplete Scorecard. What Scorecard is Your Company Playing to? Is It the Right Scorecard?

To use the table, place current metrics in the appropriate box or use the matrix to brainstorm new metrics. For example, a quality metric for the total organization might be market share. A delivery metric might be timeliness or time to delivery. A cost metric might be operational cost. See Table 3.8 for a completed example.

	Performance Areas		
	Quality (Better)	Delivery (Faster)	Cost (Lower)
Organization			
Product			
Process			
People			

Table 3.7 A Scorecard Worksheet for Metric Development

	Quality (Better)	Delivery (Faster)	Cost (Lower)
Organization	-Stock price -Market share -Organizational Climate	-Milestones -Timelines -Reaction Time	-Operational Cost -Advertising Cost -Materials Cost -Taxes -Budgets -Profits
Product	-Meeting Customer Needs -Customer Complaints -Reliability -Availability	-Development Time -Design Time -Design Changes	-Development Cost -Design Cost -Product Price -Lifecycle Cost -Cost of Poor Quality -Profit Margin
Process	-Defect Rate -Cpk -Customer Complaints	-Process Development time -Down Time -Daily Production Rate	-Manufacturing Cost -Cost of Poor Quality
People	-Safety Violation Rate -Absenteeism -Suggestion Rate	-Training Time -Rehabilitation Time -Learning Curve Time	-Turnover Rate -Training Cost -Legal Costs -Absentee Costs -Ergonomic Costs -Benefit Costs

Table 3.8 KBM Performance Scorecard

We not only need to develop the right metrics but we must also implement a strategy to hold managers accountable for these metrics. Note that the scorecard system will drive the organization in a specific direction. This powerful tool should not be implemented without careful thought, because people "play" for what's on the scorecard. It is also worth noting that once we decide on our scorecard and how to track it, we need to ensure that everyone keeps accurate data!

Another key issue related to metrics is the improvement rate goal. Author Loyd Eskildson cites inadequate goals as a major reason for failed improvement programs. He mentions that "Motorola, Harley-Davidson, Hewlett Packard, Xerox, and others initiated their quality transformation with dramatic, challenging goals for the short term and attained impressive results." He states that to improve the odds of success, we must "establish demanding, customer-focused improvement goals."

In our experience many organizations have no goals for their improvement metrics. If they do have goals, the goals are often either not challenging enough, such as 10% improvement per year, or else they are a flat goal such as 95% on time delivery. The problem with flat goals is that once they are met there is no motivation to go beyond. The way one of our clients addressed this was to set a goal of 10 fold reduction in defect levels every two years.

The intent of aggressive goal setting is to drive culture change. In this case the change was to adopt a mindset for finding different and better ways to do things in order to meet the improvement goal–not to work harder to achieve the goal. They also had a goal to reduce cycle time by a factor of 10 every five years. In other words, if the time from when an order is placed until it is shipped is now twenty days, five years from now the time from placement to shipping should be two days. In order to meet aggressive goals it takes commitment from all levels of the organization, but the goals are crucial. Every measurement chart should have a goal line on it to determine if the improvement rate goals are being met. See Figures 3.11a and 3.11b for a graphic example of aggressive (stretch) goals.

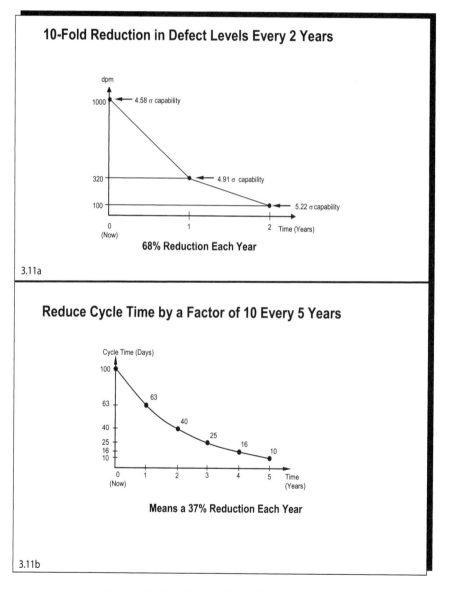

Figure 3.11 Example of Stretch Goals

13. How much waste does your company have? That is, what is the company's Cost of Waste or Cost of Poor Quality, both in raw currency amounts and also in percent of revenue? Is it getting better, staying the same, or getting worse? How much of that waste exists or originates in your area of responsibility?

Most companies, leaders, managers, and employees are not able to quantify the Cost Of Poor Quality (COPQ) in their area because they have not identified the sources of waste, scrap, and rework. And those that have estimated their COPQ seldom have a realistic value based on all areas of waste. If you don't know where you are today, how can you estimate how much you've saved tomorrow (i.e., what is your return on investment)?

"About one-third of what we do in this country consists of redoing what we did before. Chronic waste is enormous. Defects are like alligators and we're up to our hips in alligators. We keep shooting them, and they keep coming back. Why? Because we aren't planning properly. All we do is plan ways to shoot the alligators. We need to plan so we can eliminate them altogether."

J.M. Juran

Let's look at a picture of what has been happening in companies across the globe. Consider Figure 3.12a where the price of any product or service is driven by profits and total cost to produce or provide. In Figure 3.12b we see that the total cost to produce can be broken into two categories: (1) cost associated with doing the right things right the first time and (2) waste or non-value added costs, also referred to as the Cost of Poor Quality or COPQ. According to quality gurus such as Deming, Juran, etc., the percentage of COPQ in most companies is 20-40% of the total sales. Now consider Figure 3.12c where a competitor or customer-driven fixed cost or possibly budget cuts have mandated a lower price. The company represented by Figure 3.12d has responded to the new lowered price by laying off one half of its work force and/or selling off non-profitable assets, but it has done very little to cut the COPQ. This response is typical of many companies as seen on the news or read about in newspapers over the last decade. The company that will survive global markets well into the twenty-first century is depicted in Figure 3.12e. It has attacked and cut its COPQ significantly. The key to competitiveness and survival is tied to reducing the 20% to 40% waste due to poor quality, high cycle times, long development times, non-value added activities, high defect rates (or low yields), excessive inventories, duplicated efforts, transfer problems, changes, poorly optimized processes, etc. The latter approach is more difficult in the short term, but it is the only way to long-term profitability and competitiveness.

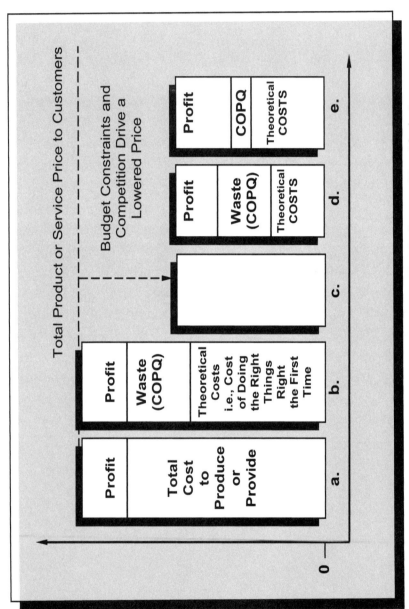

Figure 3.12 Maintaining Profits in a Highly Competitive Market

---

14. Do you have a plan that will, one year from now, show evidence that you made a difference? And what do you predict that evidence will show?

If we don't have a plan to measure impact on the company's bottom line, our apathy suggests a "will to lose" which will be a self-fulfilling prophecy. There are indeed valuable projects that will not necessarily target financial benefit realization, but if these become the rule rather than the exception, the improvement philosophy will ultimately pass away. We must never forget that the language of business is money. For most readers of this text, our job security is in our own hands. We can and must make a difference. So that we don't overestimate or underestimate our worth to the company, plan on developing a way to measure our impact on the company's bottom line. It's for our own benefit, as well as for the benefit of our company.

As a final note, be committed to play the game forever! Don't give up even when it gets frustrating. A knowledge based philosophy will last forever. It will help you add value to society and make a difference in peoples' lives. Ultimately, that's what improvement is all about. Develop a plan for answering these 14 questions and keep the faith!

Chapter 4

STRATEGIES FOR IMPROVING PERFORMANCE

"Every prudent man acts out of knowledge...."
Proverbs 13:16

Better products and services, delivered faster and at lower cost, don't just happen. We must have a plan or strategy for finding the opportunities for improvement, implementing the change, and following up. These strategies are the roadmap to increased productivity, market share, and profitability. Common sense suggests a balanced approach to implementing organizational, product, service, and process improvements. Corporate leadership is obviously concerned with short-term, as well as long-term, effects on the bottom line. Therefore, any performance improvement strategy must be robust enough to meet both needs. We cannot be so naïve as to suggest that long-term improvement of products, services, and processes is the only focus. If we don't deliver products or perform services in the short-term, there will be no short-term bottom line and perhaps no long-term bottom line either.

Chapter 3 presented a knowledge based philosophy for improving performance. This is the "what" of Knowledge Based Management. Now we need to look at the "how," which is the subject of this chapter. Please see Figure 4.1. Realizing the need to meet short-term requirements, we present this chapter as a guide for improving performance whenever and wherever opportunities exist. We will present several improvement strategies that have gained prominence over the years. As we progress through this chapter and the following ones, the astute reader will also be able to see the trends that have been occurring in the evolution of performance improvement strategies.

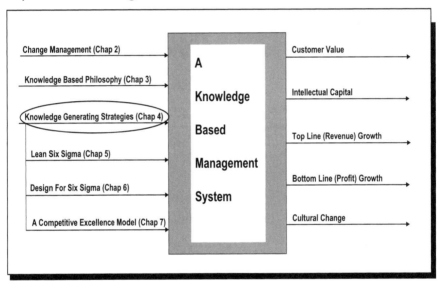

Figure 4.1 KBM IPO Diagram

PDCA/FOCUS

Most of today's powerful improvement strategies have their roots in the quality movement. One of the early strategies that gained widespread acceptance and is still in use today is the continuous improvement strategy developed by Dr. Walter Shewhart. He referred to it as the **PLAN-DO-CHECK-ACT** or **PDCA** cycle which is illustrated in Figure 4.2. We present it here as a building block to bigger and better things.

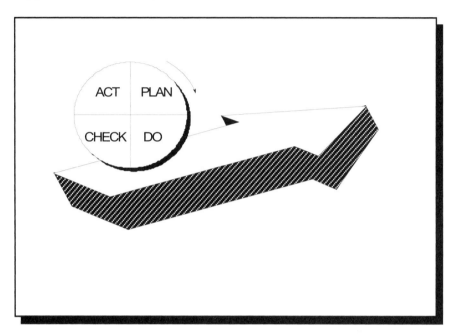

Figure 4.2 Shewhart Cycle

In later years, W. Edwards Deming, who worked and studied under Shewhart, used the term **Study** in place of **Check**, and these have become known as the Shewhart and Deming cycles. One of the more important aspects of a cycle is that it is continuous. This was by design as its emphasis is on *continuous* improvement and that any effective process improvement strategy should be iterative in nature. Both of these gurus believed that the elimination of process problems must occur in a phased, continuous cycle.

Simply stated, we first **plan** the improvement; then we **do** it; next we **check** some measurement to ensure it worked; and finally, we put it into **act**ion. Each phase of the cycle can be further described in more detail as:

PLAN

Identify and prioritize all possible processes. Then select the specific process to be improved. Map out the process using flow diagrams. Define the problem by clearly stating **what** it is, **where** and **when** it occurs, and how customer satisfaction can be measured using some process output. Analyze the process to identify possible causes of the process problem and focus on the most likely cause(s). Propose process improvement(s). Develop a data collection strategy.

DO

Develop Standard Operating Procedures (SOPs), and try out proposed improvement(s) on a small scale in a controlled environment. Monitor the improved process and document the result with data.

CHECK

Collect and analyze data to determine if the proposed improvements result in improved performance, lower cost, and reduced cycle time. Confirm results on a large scale. Use data to measure the amount of improvement.

ACT

Implement effective process changes by integrating them into the existing system of processes. Document all the improvement efforts.

Many companies that use the PDCA cycle as their performance improvement strategy find it difficult to jump start, because identifying, defining, and scoping a problem are typically not easy tasks. A strategy referred to as FOCUS is often used in breaking the "Planning" phase of the PDCA cycle into smaller components. Figure 4.3 is an outline of how FOCUS and PDCA can be used together.

Figure 4.3 Relationship Between FOCUS and PDCA

The Steps for FOCUS are as follows:

Step 1:   Find a process to improve.

Where are the opportunities for improvement? They should be defined in terms of Cost Of Poor Quality (COPQ), not just in terms of failure rates; and this may necessitate the collection of data at this point. Sometimes it is best to gain confidence by attacking a simple problem and documenting the success. However, it will eventually be necessary to attack the hard problems. If a company is measuring its critical processes, knows where the variability is coming from, and can identify the costs associated with poor quality, then it will have little difficulty in prioritizing opportunities for improvement.

Step 2:   Organize a team that knows the process.

The team should include the process owner, customers (internal and external), people with knowledge of the process, and perhaps a facilitator. The team will need to establish meeting times, milestones, objectives and assign duties.

Step 3:   Clarify current knowledge of the process.

It is almost impossible to improve a process that is not well defined. Make sure everyone is using the same terminology, understands the objective, and knows how the process works. The time spent in building a good process flow diagram can often be the most beneficial in the improvement cycle.

Step 4:   Understand causes of process variation.

Causes of variability are the major culprits of high COPQ. Processes that have been documented with data can be observed before and after the process changes have been implemented. The tough part is identifying causes for the variability. This may come from observation, from a brainstorming session, or from a designed experiment.

Step 5:   Select the process improvement.

Once we understand the problem, we need to select a solution. This involves weighing the cost of the improvement versus the benefit.

   While there are some organizations that still use PDCA/FOCUS as their improvement strategy, quite honestly, it has been replaced by more modern methods which we will present and discuss in detail. However, almost all of the concepts contained in PDCA/FOCUS have carried over to the more powerful strategies, and that is why we present PDCA/FOCUS here. One fundamental concept that carries over is that of a process, which is a key building block in all improvement strategies.

The Critical Link to Knowledge

The reasons processes are so important are that they are the key components of larger structures like products, services, and value streams or ecosystems, and that measurements can be attached to processes. Thus, it behooves us to define a process, which we characterize as a blending of inputs to achieve some desired output. We show this definition graphically in Figure 4.4 which is a very "generic" Input-Process-Output (IPO) diagram. The outputs shown in this very high level IPO diagram are the **physical** outputs of a process. Almost every activity undertaken can be classified as performing a service, producing a product, or completing a task because these are the things we do.

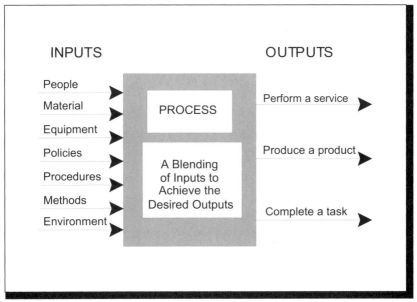

Figure 4.4 Generic IPO Diagram

However, for measurement purposes, we need to get to a finer level of granularity so that we can attach measurements to the outputs (and inputs). For example, we need to be able to determine how well we performed the service, how long did it take, how much did it cost, etc. In other words, we need to define the outputs (and inputs, if possible) in measurable terms. Examples of specific output measures might be: 1) for a billing process we measure the time to complete a bill and the percent of bills with errors; 2) for a machining process we measure the inner and outer diameters of a machined part; 3) for a composite material process we measure the material porosity and tensile strength; 4) for a mail sorting process we measure the time it takes to sort the mail and the proportion of damaged mail; and 5) for a software installation/operational process we measure computation time, number of errors, and system availability, among other key measures.

Specific IPO diagrams for the billing, machining, composite material, mail sorting and software processes (including key inputs) are shown in Figures 4.5, 4.6, 4.7, 4.8, and 4.9, respectively.

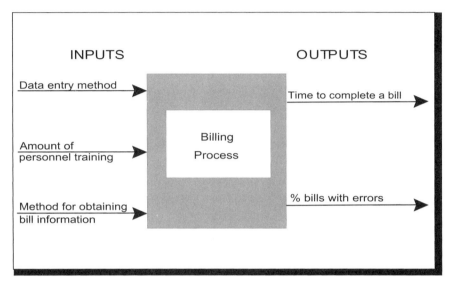

Figure 4.5 Billing Process Diagram

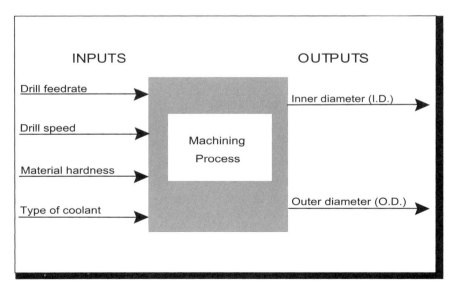

Figure 4.6 Machining Process Diagram

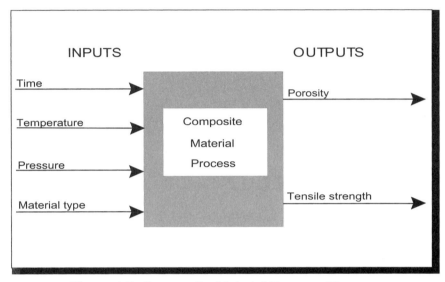

Figure 4.7 Composite Material Process Diagram

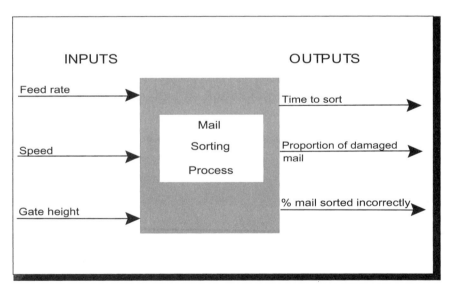

Figure 4.8 Mail Sorting Process Diagram

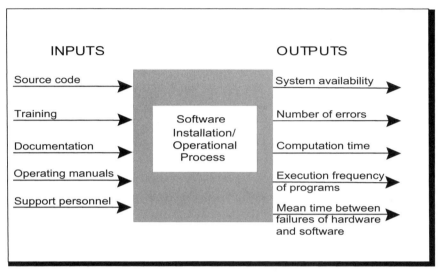

Figure 4.9 Installation/Operational Phase of the Software Lifecycle

To fully understand our processes and make continuous improvements necessitates the gathering, displaying and analysis of process data. The proper emphasis on measurement can probably not be put any more succinctly than the way Lord Kelvin expressed it over a century ago (1891):

> *"...When you can measure what you are speaking about and express it in numbers, you know something about it, but when you cannot express it in numbers, your knowledge is of a meagre and unsatisfactory kind."*
>
> *Lord Kelvin*

The bottom line is we don't know what we don't know and we won't know unless we measure. The IPO diagram for a process provides us the basic building block for measurement and understanding.

According to Peter Scholtes, author of **The Team Handbook,** there are generally six sources of problems associated with process knowledge. These are shown in Table 4.1.

---

1. **Lack of understanding of how a process actually works.**

2. **Lack of knowledge of how a process should work.**

3. **Errors and/or mistakes in executing process steps.**

4. **Practices which fail to recognize the need for preventative measures, such as maintenance or training.**

5. **Non-value added steps, activities which consume time and resources, but do not add value to the product or service.**

6. **Variation in inputs and outputs.**

Table 4.1 Process Knowledge Problems

Obviously, effective process improvement methods must be able to identify and eliminate these six types of problems.

A Knowledge Generating Strategy

Whether called PDCA/FOCUS or something else, improvement strategies have been around for many years. Sometimes they work and sometimes they don't. What makes one organization successful while another fails at implementing the strategy? As previously stated, one of the leading causes for failure is poor leadership and management support. It is easy to say that leadership should support its employees if it is serious about improving performance. But leadership support must be more than providing money and time for training or giving a hearty "pat on the back" for a job well done. Conversely, employees need to be held accountable and provide a return on the investment that leadership has made in providing the training, resources, and time to give employees the wherewithal to produce the desired results. What is missing in most improvement strategies is the barebones ability to create the right knowledge at the right time for the right people. This is the missing link for obtaining return on investment from any performance improvement strategy. Please reference Figure 4.10.

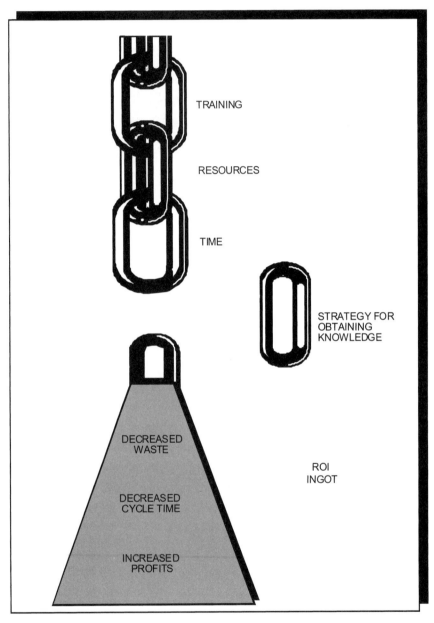

Figure 4.10 Missing Link for Obtaining ROI from an Improvement Strategy

The intent of this section is to provide leaders with something they can use immediately to bridge the gaps that may exist in their organization's knowledge generation capability. We present a set of questions called **Questions Leaders Must Ask**. These questions form a pull-system for generating the right kinds of knowledge, the kind that will allow leaders and managers to make good decisions. Any performance improvement strategy that does not include the basic building blocks for acquiring the right kind of knowledge is doomed to failure. These questions will also provide leaders the ability to think critically about their processes, products, people, and organizations. We first present the list of 14 questions, but then we go into more detail on each of the questions, providing more rationale on why these questions are so important. We encourage the reader not to skip over the details presented for each question.

Questions Leaders Must Ask
1. Which value stream are you supporting and who is the recipient of the value, i.e., who is the customer? Who is the value stream owner and who are the players or team members? How well does the team work together?
2. Within the value stream, which process or processes have the highest priority for improvement? Show me the data that led to this conclusion.
(Continued on next page)

Table 4.2 Questions Leaders Must Ask

For the process or processes targeted for improvement:

3. How is the process performed? How does the value flow? What activity is value added and what is non-value added?

4. What are the process performance measures, i.e., how will we gauge if a process is improving? Why did we choose those? How accurate and precise is the measurement system? Show me the data.

5. What are the customer-driven requirements or specifications for all of the performance measures? Are the process performance measures in control and how capable is the process? Show me the data. What are the improvement goals for the value stream or process performance measures?

6. What kinds of waste and cost of poor quality exist in the value stream or process and what is the financial and/or customer impact? Show me the data.

7. What are all the sources of variability in the value stream or process and which of those do we control? How do we control them and what is our method of documenting and maintaining this control? Show me the data.

8. Are any sources of waste or variability supplier-dependent? If so, what are they, who are the suppliers, and how are we working together to eliminate waste and variability? Show me the data.

(Continued on next page)

Table 4.2 Questions Leaders Must Ask

9. What are the key input variables that affect the average and standard deviation of the measures of performance? How do you know this? Show me the data.

10. What are the relationships between the measures of performance and the key input variables? Do any of the key input variables interact? How do you know for sure? Show me the data.

11. What settings or values for the key input variables will optimize the measures of performance? How do you know this? Show me the data.

12. For the optimal settings of the key input variables, what kind of variability still exists in the performance measures? How do you know? Show me the data.

13. Have we implemented a process flow and control system to sustain the gains and continuously improve the process? Show me the data.

14. How much improvement has the value stream or process shown in the past six months? How much time and/or money have our efforts saved the company? Show me the data.

Table 4.2 Questions Leaders Must Ask

Our claim is that if leadership asks its people the right questions, ensures its people are trained in the best practices to answer these questions, and if the organization provides a climate where people are motivated to improve performance while at the same time holding them accountable for results, then return on investment will take place in the form of better products and services, delivered faster and at lower cost. The direct by-products of this approach will be increased customer value, increased revenue and profit margin, improved intellectual capital, and desired cultural change.

We now examine each of these **Questions Leaders Must Ask** in more detail.

---

1. **Which value stream are you supporting and who is the recipient of the value, i.e., who is the customer? Who is the value stream owner and who are the players or team members? How well does the team work together?**

Simply stated, a value stream is a set of activities that deliver value to a customer. From order to delivery is an example of a value stream. On the surface, these seem like simple questions, and for most employees they should be easy to answer. However, we have seen organizations where the answers to these questions are not always readily understood. Part of a leader's responsibility is to direct and support his/her people and that includes making sure they can answer these questions. If we ask the first question and find people struggling to answer it, chances are we have not communicated job responsibilities to our employees in a clear and concise manner.

For any team to function properly, it is also critical for everyone involved in a process to understand who all of the players are. Each team player must know what each person's responsibility is, to include who is ultimately responsible; that is, who's the owner of the process or value stream?

Team dynamics are also an important aspect of the knowledge gaining process. If a team does not consist of harmoniously working members who are in sync with a specific leader, there typically will be chaos. Also keep in mind that team members and/or team leaders who dominate to the point of shutting others off will hinder team performance. Likewise, team members who fail to participate or who pout after they don't get their way are not only non-functional, but can degrade team cohesiveness and performance. Leaders need to know the value of each team member's contribution and have the ability to remove a person from the team if there is no value added. The success of the improvement process very much depends on the ability of management to foster teamwork and the team problem solving process. In our experience the companies that successfully manage the team problem solving process are the ones that obtain the best ROI from their improvement effort.

> **"Only by drawing on the combined brainpower of all its employees can a firm face up to the turbulence and constraints of today's environment."**
>
> *Konosuke Matsushita*
>
> *Matsushita Electric Industrial Co*

One organization having great success with the team problem solving process is Freudenberg-NOK. In an article in "Rubber and Plastic News," CEO Joseph C. Day said that "Freudenberg-NOK spends $750,000 annually on the improvement team process and gets a ten to twelve fold return on investment. The company has…

more than doubled its sales to $600 million using about 40 percent less [floor] space and the same number of employees working just five days a week rather than 6½ days..." Obviously, the team problem solving process can be very effective if implemented properly.

The team problem solving process can be thought of as the engine that drives the improvement process. The successful teams in all areas within an organization will be using the tools to answer the questions that leaders need to ask. This is what makes Knowledge Based Management work.

You will notice that a few times in this text we reference job security as an outcome of the performance improvement process. This is a crucial result that leadership needs to plan for. It stands to reason that no one will work to improve productivity if that person expects to be laid off as a result. If a project improves productivity and eliminates the need for one person in an area, leadership needs to make a commitment to find that person another position. To lay that person off would be suicide to the improvement process.

*Consider the following excerpts from a "Chicago Tribune" review of the book **The Loyalty Effect: The Hidden Force Behind Growth, Profits, and Lasting Value** by Frederick F. Reichheld.*

1. Revenues and market share grow as the best customers are swept into the company's business, building repeat sales and referrals.

2. Sustainable growth enables the firm to attract and retain the best employees while consistently delivering superior value to customers. That in turn increases employees' loyalty by giving them pride and satisfaction in their work.

3. Loyal long term employees learn on the job how to reduce costs and improve performance, which further enriches the customer-value proposition and generates superior productivity.

4. Upward-spiraling productivity coupled with increased efficiency of dealing with loyal customers generates the kind of cost advantage that is difficult for competitors to match.

It is clear that companies successful in the improvement process can expect both increased revenues and market share. This makes it reasonable to commit to not reducing the work force as an outcome of an improvement project that results in increased efficiencies.

"Teamwork is about getting 25 guys playing for the name on the front of their uniforms rather than the name on the back."

Tommy Lasorda
Los Angeles Dodgers

---

2. Within the value stream, which process or processes have the highest priority for improvement? Show me the data that led to this conclusion.

Many people in industry are stressed out from working hard. Their plate (so to speak) is full and they are juggling many responsibilities. In such an environment, the only way to keep from burning out and/or going insane is to have a clear understanding of the priorities. It is leadership's responsibility to set the priorities. Several things to consider in setting priorities are based on the scorecard philosophy discussed in Chapter 3. A list of further considerations should include the following:

Early Phases of Product/Service Development

1. Marketing Strategies
2. Customer Needs
3. Cost of Delayed Market Entry
4. Cost of Possible Recall after Market Entry
5. Projected Sales
6. Profit Margin
7. Where in the Lifecycle the Activity is Located

Later Phases of Product/Service Development

1. Yield
2. Cycle Times
3. Cost of Poor Quality
4. Customer Complaints
5. Profit Margin
6. Where in the Lifecycle the Activity is Located

When several different activities compete for limited resources, a comparison based on data collected on the above metrics will be helpful. This comparative analysis can help an individual and/or team identify the critical activities versus those less critical. Too often we have seen the selection of processes to be "reengineered" based on gut feel, rather than any kind of comparative analysis based on hard facts and data. Most organizations typically do not have the resources to attack every problem simultaneously. Hence, good decision-making at this point can and should lead to greater return on investment from the resources expended.

It is also important to note that many failed improvement efforts come as a result of trying to solve too big of a problem and/or trying to improve downstream activities when upstream ones are out of control.

FOR THE PROCESS OR PROCESSES TARGETED FOR IMPROVEMENT:

> **3. How is the process performed? How does the value flow? What activity is value added and what is non-value added?**

A host of problems can result when we convince ourselves that this step is something everyone already understands. Especially when dealing with complex processes, it is not uncommon for each person on a team to have a different view of how an activity takes place. If all the players involved are not in agreement on how an activity is performed, there will inevitably be excess waste and variation. Extraneous variation generates fires which in turn generate fire-fighting. Although fire-fighting may appear necessary in the short term, fire prevention is required to improve the bottom line in the long term.

The best approach to basic problem solving is to first map out every major step in an activity. Then carefully break down each major step into exactly how the process is performed. Although this question needs to be answered with words describing each step, the more we can use graphics the better the communication.

Failing to satisfactorily answer this question leads to aborted attempts at acquiring knowledge and the unsuccessful transitioning of an activity from:

i) small scale to large scale

ii) site to site

iii) one generation product/service to the next generation

iv) supplier to customer

Oftentimes the simplest of tools like a process flow diagram can reveal ways to reduce cycle time, defects, and non-value added activities.

> **"If we can't agree on how to do something, how can we all be doing it the best way?"**
>
> *Anonymous*

> **4. What are the process performance measures, i.e., how will we gauge if a process is improving? Why did we choose those? How accurate and precise is the measurement system? Show me the data.**

In order to improve (and to prove that we have improved) a process there will have to be some measure(s) of performance. We have referred to these previously as process outputs or CTCs (Critical to Customer). Since what we measure will drive the entire improvement process, it is paramount that we measure the right thing. Measures of performance should somehow represent a metric related to customer needs. For example, if our customers are telling us "they don't like to wait on hold," then "hold time" would be an appropriate metric to track. If they say, "I hate getting bounced around to multiple people or voice messages," then "number of transitions needed to reach the right person" may be an appropriate metric. If what we are measuring cannot be correlated to a customer (internal or external), it is probably a non-value added measurement. A good starting point for metric development is to answer the following questions:

1. *Who are my internal and external customers?*
2. *What are my customers' needs?*

3. *What measures of performance are related to those needs and which of these will give me feedback on how well the customer needs are being met?*

4. *How can I prioritize the measures of performance listed in (3) above?*

Many organizations, particularly those in the service sector, struggle with what it is that they should measure. Since almost every customer need is related in some way to cost, schedule (time), or quality, we suggest the following process—a matrix development approach—to generate potentially valid metrics. Here is how it works:

Step 1: *Identify the critical processes that are essential for the success of the company.*

Step 2: *Build a critical process/performance criteria matrix as shown in Table 4.3.*

Step 3: *Fill in the definition portion of the matrix by defining each process in detail. Note that the process flow diagram can be used for this purpose.*

Step 4: *Brainstorm potential factors that affect the performance   criteria. Quality, time, and cost criteria are shown in Table 4.3, but other criteria such as safety, ergonomics, and environment could also apply.*

Step 5: *Select potential measures from the cause and effect diagram.*

Note that this process combines the use of some very basic tools: process flow, brainstorming, cause and effect diagram, and a matrix to synergize the effect of each of the tools individually.

Critical Processes		Performance Criteria			
Name	Definition	Quality/Accuracy	Time	Cost	
Verification Testing		Quality/Accuracy	Time	Cost	
Field Support		Quality/Accuracy	Time	Cost	
	· · ·	· · ·	· · ·	· · ·	

Table 4.3 Critical Process / Performance Criteria Matrix

Another important part of this question is addressing our measurement system. We must carefully decide on how to measure our activity, the cost of the measurement system, and most importantly, the accuracy and precision of the measurement system. If we are making decisions based on data, we must make sure the data has integrity. A simple Measurement System Analysis (MSA) can accomplish this. Gathering data on a process is a process in itself, and care should be taken to make this process as efficient as possible, while maintaining the integrity and validity of the data. Operational definitions (for example, definition of a defect) are of utmost importance and could have a significant impact on the measurement system.

---

5. What are the customer-driven requirements or specifications for all of the performance measures? Are the process performance measures in control and how capable is the process? Show me the data. What are the improvement goals for the value stream or process performance measures?

Using customer needs to derive the measures of performance (outputs) allows us to more easily determine optimal values and acceptable limits for our outputs. These acceptable limits are in reality the customer driven specifications. Ideally we should not arbitrarily set customer specifications. For example, consider a pilot production phase where we make some (3 to 30) prototypes and measure their individual parameters. Suppose one particular parameter, call it y, has 15 measured values stacked on a number line, as shown in Figure 4.11. We then use software to compute the mean or average value ($\bar{y}$) and the standard deviation (σ or sigma) from the set of values. The spread from ($\bar{y}$ - 3σ) to ($\bar{y}$ + 3σ), as shown in Figure 4.11, *represents the natural tolerances of the parameter y. If we set the specification limits for y at ($\bar{y}$ - 3σ) and ($\bar{y}$ + 3σ), these are in reality statistical limits. However, these limits do not necessarily reflect the customer requirements.*

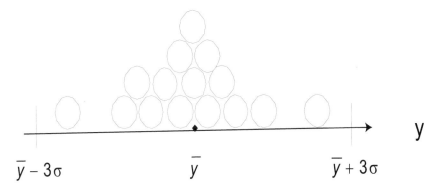

$$\bar{y} - 3\sigma \qquad\qquad \bar{y} \qquad\qquad \bar{y} + 3\sigma$$

Figure 4.11 Measured Values of Parameter y

The customer should, in fact, be a part of the specification setting process. That means we need to dialogue with the customer. For example, what kind of "hold time" is a customer willing to accept? There will be variation between customers, which needs to be considered in setting specifications. Keep in mind that some customers do not fully understand their needs or the capability of state-of-the-art technologies. Compromises may need to be made. Thus, the relationship between the supplier and customer should be one of open communications.

Another approach to setting targets and specifications is to benchmark the industry on similar products/services. This insures that the targets and specifications we select will be competitive. However, it does not necessarily mean that our process or product is competitive. To determine how good or bad the current performance is requires us to look at how the voice of the process (VOP) compares to the voice of the customer (VOC). In other words, we assess the process capability. To drive improvement of the capability measures, management and teams must work together to develop effective stretch goals and be held accountable for these goals.

While capability tells us how good the process is by comparing the VOP with the VOC, process control refers only to the "stability" of the process and it needs only the VOP data to do so. Unfortunately, many leaders do not understand the difference between the terms "control" and "capability" as they are used in the context of improvement. Hence, many faulty decisions are made because "control" does not imply "capability," and "capability" does not imply "control." We could possibly have both, only one, or neither; and knowing what we have is critical to good decision making.

Proper goal setting for improvement is also dependent on our knowledge of capability and control. We seldom hit what we don't aim for, so in order to make our goals SMART (Specific, Measurable, Achievable, Relevant, and Timely), we must have a good handle on both the capability and control aspects of the measures we are trying to improve.

---

6. What kinds of waste and cost of poor quality exist in the value stream or process and what is the financial and/or customer impact? Show me the data.

Unless we can place a monetary value on an improvement effort, the impetus for an improvement strategy will be short-lived. The importance of answering this question cannot be overstated, because it is tied to the "need" for change in an organization. And if this "need" can be expressed in the language of leadership and management, namely financial terms, it will have a much better chance of gaining the priority required by leadership for attacking it. We now provide a common way to categorize cost of poor quality and waste. Table 4.4 lists the five major categories of Cost of Poor Quality (COPQ).

Cost of Poor Quality
• Internal Failure Costs
• External Failure Costs
• Appraisal Costs
• Prevention Costs
• Lost Opportunity Costs

Table 4.4 Major Cost of Poor Quality (COPQ) Categories

*Internal failure costs are those costs that are incurred **prior** to product or service delivery/shipment to the customer. These costs include such things as accounting errors, excess travel expenses, premium freight (when not needed), failure reviews, employee turnover, rework, and scrap. Taichi Ohno's infamous types of waste shown in Table 4.5 also fall in this category.*

The Seven Types of Waste	
1. **Transportation**:	movement of goods/services produced
2. **Inventory**:	any partial or fully developed goods or services
3. **Motion**:	extra steps or data entry performed by resources
4. **Waiting**:	any delay that leads to idle time
5. **Over-production**:	producing more than is needed
6. **Over-processing**:	doing more than is needed; adding more features than are used
7. **Defects**:	any product or service that doesn't meet customer requirements/specifications

Table 4.5 Ohno's Seven Types of Waste

*External failure costs are those that occur **after** the product or service is in the presence of the customer. Some common examples include pricing errors, recall costs, returned goods, warranty claims, bad debts and customer complaint investigation.*

Appraisal costs are those associated with measuring, evaluating, or auditing products or services to ensure conformance to quality standards and performance requirements. These are costs associated with conformance. Some examples include document checking, financial audits, in-process testing or inspection, receiving inspection, and quality control costs.

Prevention costs are the costs of all activities specially designed to prevent defects (poor quality) in products and services. These occur prior to production and are aimed at preventing defects before they occur. Examples include contract reviews, field trials, forecasting, personnel reviews, supplier quality reviews, and vendor evaluation/selection.

The last category, the cost of lost opportunity, is typically the most difficult to measure directly but can be measured via activities like expected value analysis, etc. Examples in this category include competition beating us to market, delayed market entry, lost customer goodwill/sales, lost market share, and reliability issues.

One of the major reasons we want to get a handle on these costs is to show that the "Cost of Doing Nothing" (CODN) is NOT zero.

---

7. What are all the sources of variability in the value stream or process and which of those do we control? How do we control them and what is our method of documenting and maintaining this control? Show me the data.

By now we should know all the outputs to be measured, their targets and specifications, along with good estimates of the cost of waste and poor quality. The next obvious step is to identify every known variable that can possibly affect these critical measures. The more complex the product/service or process (activity) the larger the number of sources of variability and the more crucial it is to answer this question. Some practitioners use the complexity of their processes as an excuse for not trying to answer this question. Common sense should indicate that highly complex processes have so many variables in them that the brain cannot keep up with them day to day. Therefore, it is extremely important that they all be formally documented.

To ensure that all the variables are listed, it is best to form categories of sources of variation and to thoroughly think through each step in the process (activity). It is also important to list each source of variability in terms of a specific variable and not use general or abstract terms. For example, instead of listing "environment" we should specify the following variables: temperature, humidity, pressure, altitude, wind speed, etc.

Theoretically, if we know all the sources of variability and tightly control each one, the outputs should be in control with low variability. Conversely, if we are not aware of some major sources of variability and/or they are left uncontrolled, we can expect the outputs to be out of control and/or vulnerable to excessive variability. Therefore, answering this question is necessary to control our processes and to reduce variability.

This is also a good place to brainstorm all possible failure modes, their effects and their causes. We should list every possible cause for failure in order to prioritize them and to prepare for finding a way to "foolproof" the process from these failures. The process of listing all the sources of variability and/or failure modes will not likely be complete the first time we do it. Therefore, this question needs to be re-visited, and any changes need to be documented and dated so that we will always know the current version used to answer this question.

To successfully control the various sources of variability or failure, we need to develop simple, low-cost Standard Operating Procedures (SOPs) for holding most of these variables constant and for foolproofing most of the causes of failure and waste. These SOPs should be clearly stated and all employees trained and motivated to understand and comply with the SOPs. This is a critical step toward getting any process/activity into control and/or preventing product/service failures. It is important that these documents that delineate all the variables and the SOPs that control these variables be "living" documents. That is, they will change over time. We highly encourage SOPs to have sunset clauses. That is, they will go away unless they are improved or revalidated. When asking the question "do you have SOPs?," we often hear "of course we have SOPs, but I like to do it my way." The Frank Sinatra approach, or "my way," is in vogue. If "your way" is the best, then we all ought to be doing it that way. Having sunset clauses on all SOPs forces us to improve/revalidate the SOP.

Many believe that the construction of and strict adherence to a set of SOPs for the purpose of controlling critical variables is a violation of the principles of ingenuity, creativity, innovation and, in general, the empowerment of people. Certainly ingenuity, creativity, and innovation are desperately needed in the discovery of critical factors which affect our products/services and processes/activities. In fact, using SOPs to control excessive variation will provide the practitioners more time to be creative and innovative, which is exactly why we use them. However, when these enviable human attributes are left to flounder in an unorganized and poorly managed scenario, the most likely result is chaos and fire-fighting, as depicted in Figure 4.12.

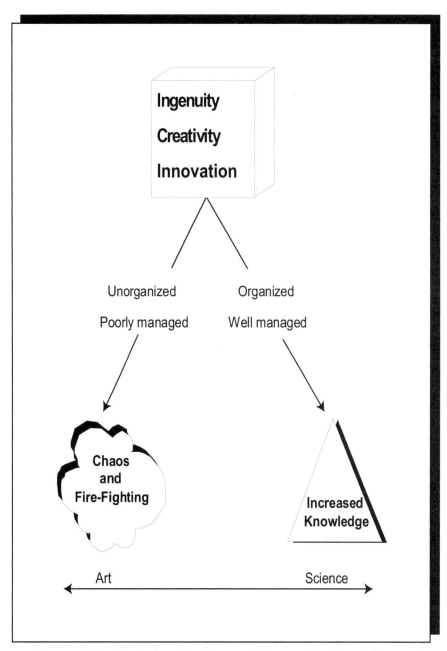

Figure 4.12 Capturing the Power of Ingenuity, Creativity, and Innovation

On the other hand, if ingenuity, creativity, and innovation are properly harnessed in an organized and well managed scenario, we can make unbelievable advances in gaining knowledge. Knowledge Based Management is the key to transforming the art of management into a science.

Significant return on investment has been made in all types of products/services and processes through a concentrated effort in answering Questions 3-7. These questions constitute a structured approach to basic problem solving and are the key essentials to practicing the scientific method.

The documentation for the most current answers to these questions should be placed in an electronic or hard copy notebook to serve as a library of product/service/process knowledge. The more precise and specific the answers are, the greater the level of knowledge. Any transfer of technology should also include the transfer of this notebook. Furthermore, the certification, registration, or qualification process under umbrellas such as ISO-9000, QS-9000, D1-9000, Quality Systems Review, Process Validation, Process Analytical Technology, Process Characterization, etc., will be greatly facilitated by simply repackaging the knowledge contained in this notebook.

---

8. Are any sources of waste or variability supplier-dependent? If so, what are they, who are the suppliers, and how are we working together to eliminate waste and variability? Show me the data.

If our suppliers are providing us with highly variable materials and services, it may be difficult to magically develop product/services or processes without excessive variability in our critical performance measures. It is best to find some key measures for our vendors' products and to produce histograms, run charts or control charts to evaluate the consistency of our incoming materials and services.

If we have evidence of excessive variation due to a specific supplier, it is advised that we help the supplier answer Questions 1 through 7 in order to improve the processes. This can be a very sensitive issue and each situation may have to be handled differently.

In general, there are six options for handling vendor variability problems:

i.   *work with the vendors, helping them implement performance improvement;*

ii. *perform incoming inspection to selectively screen out non-conforming products or services;*

iii. *design an experiment to find a way to make the process robust (insensitive to vendor variation);*

iv. *find a better vendor;*

v.   *verify, validate, and possibly change the requirements;*

vi. *redesign the product.*

Research and experience shows that option (i) is the most effective in gaining long-term ROI. Working with vendors, training with them, and doing joint performance improvement projects with them has proven to be one of the best ways to optimize value streams for customers.

> **9. What are the key input variables that affect the average and standard deviation of the measures of performance? How do you know this? Show me the data.**

In order to improve the measures of performance (outputs) for our process, knowledge of the variables which shift the average and/or standard deviation of the output is required.

The objective for almost any measure of performance will be to either:

1. *maximize the average value with low variation,*

2. *minimize the average value with low variation, or*

3. *achieve a target for the average value with low variation.*

To accomplish this task we need to know which inputs can be used to adjust the average output up or down and which inputs can be used to adjust the variation down. When this information is not available from prior knowledge we will either need to analyze historical data or design an experiment. Certainly, prior knowledge, experience and a literature review can greatly reduce the number of inputs that will have to be investigated via experimentation.

Collecting and analyzing historical data or designing experiments for the purpose of making improvements requires that we first successfully answer Questions 1 through 8. If we fail to address these essentials it is likely that we will not gain "knowledge" and only fuel a raging fire of "chaos." If we are in desperate need of finding inputs that lead to minimizing variation, it is worth noting that the most efficient and effective way to accomplish this task will be through a screening Design of Experiments (DOE).

> **10. What are the relationships between the measures of performance and the key input variables? Do any of the key input variables interact? How do you know for sure? Show me the data.**

Answering this question requires the use of historical data modeling or a modeling DOE. As stated in Question 9, either of these modeling approaches presupposes a heavy emphasis on Questions 1 through 8; otherwise, the models will not produce knowledge.

Every process has a true physical model. However, when the theory is not available to produce the true physical model, we need to go to the process itself and ask it questions. Design of Experiments (DOE) is the discipline of interrogating a process in a systematic and efficient manner for the purpose of discovering how the input factors affect the output. A properly designed experiment will produce an accurate model which should closely approximate the true physical model. Knowledge of a process at this level of detail translates into competitive advantage. Characterization, optimization, sensitivity, tolerance setting, and trade-off analysis are now possible.

> **11. What settings or values for the key input variables will optimize the measures of performance? How do you know this? Show me the data.**

Knowing the model for the average response and the model for the standard deviation of the response allows us to determine the settings for the key variables which will optimize our objectives. The term "response" as used here represents a process output or a specific performance measure. By having the models, we have the necessary knowledge to optimize. Furthermore, if costs about the input variables are known, the models can be used to accomplish cost/benefit trade-off analysis. Without the models, our knowledge of our products, services and/or associated processes is limited. Thus, we also limit our ability to make the best decisions to achieve better, faster, and lower cost results.

> **12. For the optimal settings of the key input variables, what kind of variability still exists in the performance measures? How do you know? Show me the data.**

Once optimal input variable settings are determined, practitioners should always validate the model through what experimenters call confirmatory runs. Confirmatory runs not only tell us if the model predicts well, but also tell us what kind of variability exists in the output (or performance measure). Before we even do confirmatory runs, the models allow us to predict what our average response should be and what the standard deviation should be when we run the process under the optimal input variable settings. If the confirmatory runs fall within the predicted interval, we say we have confirmed the model. If enough confirmation runs are performed, we can estimate the process capability.

> **"All models are wrong, but some are useful."**
>
> *George Box*

The models that are useful are the ones that have been confirmed or validated.

13. Have we implemented a process flow and control system to sustain the gains and continuously improve the process? Show me the data.

Assuming we have already answered questions 1 - 12, our "state of knowledge" should be such that we now know both the critical input variables and the critical output measures of performance. Based on this knowledge, improvements have already been made. But how will we know if we have sustained those gains over time? Furthermore, how will we know if we are continuing to improve a process that was targeted for improvement? To answer these questions, we will need to set up a system that tracks the process over time. The most useful techniques for doing this are the run chart and the control chart, because these tools allow us to track data over time.

The purpose of a Process Flow and Control System (PFCS) is to encapsulate all of the critical pieces of knowledge already generated from answering questions 1 - 12 and to put them under lock and key. That means all of the critical input and output variables must be tracked over time, i.e., put under a state of surveillance using, preferably, control charts, because control charts are more powerful than run charts. A control chart easily signals when a change has taken place in a critical variable, either output or input. This information allows the process or value stream owner to take action as needed, neither over-reacting nor under-reacting, thus providing overall stability to the management of key processes.

How often have we seen culture gobble up profitable changes produced by an improvement event? Very often. Why? The underlying change was not sustained because a PFCS was not implemented or monitored properly. In a nutshell, the PFCS provides the scorecard needed to sustain the gains and continuously improve the process.

---

14. How much improvement has the value stream or process shown in the past six months? How much time and/or money have our efforts saved the company? Show me the data.

The answer to Question 14 requires the use of a scorecard to record process improvement over time. Examples of computable measures of performance include defects per unit (dpu), cycle time, or COPQ. We would be hard pressed to convince anyone that our process has improved if our scorecard for COPQ appeared as shown in Figure 4.13. This is nothing more than random variation.

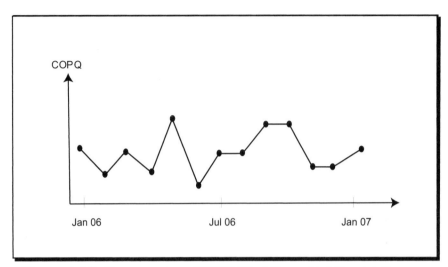

Figure 4.13 Scorecard on COPQ That Does Not Depict Process
Improvement

*On the other hand, a scorecard that looks like the one in Figure
4.14 may indeed be indicative of improvement.*

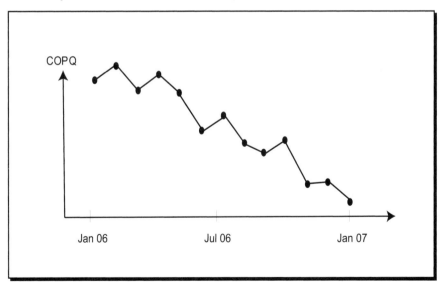

Figure 4.14 Scorecard on COPQ That May Depict Process
Improvement

We say "may be indicative" because if this is true process improvement, we will know why COPQ is going down. That is, if we were to do it all over again, it would be repeatable and we would have the documentation that links what we did with the results.

The results depicted in Figure 4.14 must be correlated with the company's bottom line. That is, we don't want optimization of one process to cause deterioration in other areas or processes of the company. Localized versus global optimization can be a problem, especially in companies where keeping score is synonymous with gathering evidence to fire someone. Management must ensure that scorecards are implemented in a way that motivates people to play to win but to do so in an ethical manner without feeling the pressure to falsify data. Advanced charting techniques can sometimes detect the presence of falsified data, but the key is to prevent this from happening in the first place. Solid knowledge about people, processes, products, and organizations is the key to an honest, ethical, and winning scorecard that generates real return on investment and enhances job security.

This concludes our discussion of each of the 14 questions that leaders need to ask. These questions represent the implementation strategy for a Knowledge Based Management system and provide leaders with something they can use immediately to promote performance improvement. Leaders who ask these questions are on track to become leaders in developing their people and improving their processes. The answers to these questions provide the knowledge which drives the actual process improvement.

Any improvement strategy that is designed to produce return on investment must be able to generate the knowledge that these 14 questions are designed to pull. The next section on Six Sigma describes a modern, powerful improvement strategy that does this very well.

Six Sigma/DMAIC

Six Sigma means different things to different people. For many who have never used it or have only heard of it, Six Sigma may be just a fad. To some, Six Sigma is a set of tools. Others think of Six Sigma as a measure of capability or possibly a philosophy or even a business strategy. But today, almost everyone who has used Six Sigma will agree that it is a very powerful improvement strategy. The Six Sigma strategy is linked to the methodology that is called DMAIC (Define, Measure, Analyze, Improve, Control), but the strategy includes more than just the DMAIC methodology. It also includes the infrastructure and critical factors that make Six Sigma implementation and deployment highly likely to be successful. Six Sigma is no longer an experimental approach to performance improvement. We know what makes it successful and can share with our readers those critical elements. The remainder of this chapter introduces the reader to Six Sigma and DMAIC and what makes it tick.

Six Sigma began in the 1980's at Motorola and the Six Sigma Research Institute. It quickly expanded to companies like Allied Signal and General Electric, whose CEOs embraced it as a disciplined, repeatable process that delivered bottom line results. The "transplantation" effect of Six Sigma has been substantial, as key executives who move from one company to another take the Six Sigma methodology and philosophy with them. There is perhaps no better example of this than what happened in 2000 when 3 senior executives left General Electric and became CEOs of companies, jumpstarting Six Sigma at 3M (Jim McNerney), Home Depot (Bob Nardelli), and Intuit (Steve Bennett). It is thus not coincidence that today 82 of the 100 leading publicly traded companies in the U.S. claim to use Six Sigma (**iSixSigma Magazine**, Nov/Dec 2006). There is no denying that Six Sigma has proven to be a superb performance improvement strategy for many companies. Reference the Appendix which shows a sampling of Six Sigma DMAIC projects and their corresponding results.

An elevator speech describing Six Sigma might go something like this: it is a customer-focused change strategy driven by market requirements and business leaders who empower teams with a powerful methodology and the best tools to leverage talent and deliver accelerated results. The goals and benefits of Six Sigma can be summarized as follows:

(1) Delivering greater value to our customers by

- Improving delivery times

- Reducing the Cost of Poor Quality (COPQ)

- Understanding and satisfying customer needs and wants

(2) Helping our company become more profitable by

- Removing wasteful and non-value added activities

- Reducing cycle times and inventories

- Growing revenue

(3) Making our own jobs and workplace better and more secure by

- Becoming more effective and efficient

- Developing valuable job skills to continuously improve performance

The repeatable, disciplined methodology that is followed to produce results is the DMAIC (Define, Measure, Analyze, Improve, Control) process. This phase gate process is shown in Figure 4.15.

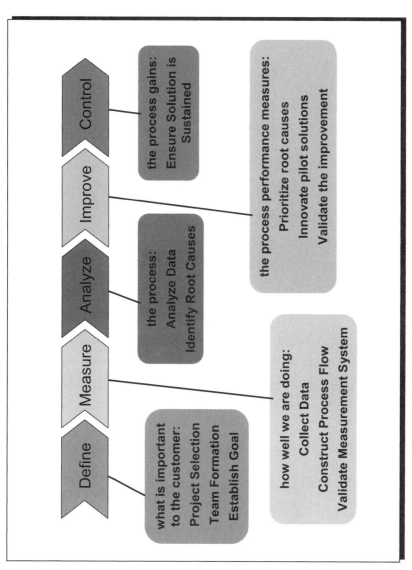

Figure 4.15 DMAIC: A Powerful Methodology

Note that the DMAIC methodology nicely imbeds the knowledge generating questions discussed earlier in this chapter as shown in Table 4.6.

Define

1. Which value stream are you supporting and who is the recipient of the value, i.e., who is the customer? Who is the value stream owner and who are the players or team members? How well does the team work together?
2. Within the value stream, which process or processes have the highest priority for improvement? Show me the data that led to this conclusion.

For the process or processes targeted for improvement,

Measure

3. How is the process performed? How does the value flow? What activity is value added and what is non-value added?
4. What are the process performance measures, i.e., how will we gauge if a process is improving? Why did we choose those? How accurate and precise is the measurement system? Show me the data.
5. What are the customer-driven requirements or specifications for all of the performance measures? Are the process performance measures in control and how capable is the process? Show me the data. What are the improvement goals for the value stream or process performance measures?

(Continued on next page)

Table 4.6 Questions Leaders Need to Ask in the DMAIC Phases

Analyze

6. What kinds of waste and cost of poor quality exist in the value stream or process and what is the financial and/or customer impact? Show me the data.

7. What are all the sources of variability in the value stream or process and which of those do we control? How do we control them and what is our method of documenting and maintaining this control? Show me the data.

8. Are any sources of waste or variability supplier-dependent? If so, what are they, who are the suppliers, and how are we working together to eliminate waste and variability? Show me the data.

9. What are the key input variables that affect the average and standard deviation of the measures of performance? How do you know this? Show me the data.

10. What are the relationships between the measures of performance and the key input variables? Do any of the key input variables interact? How do you know for sure? Show me the data.

Improve

11. What settings or values for the key input variables will optimize the measures of performance? How do you know this? Show me the data.

12. For the optimal settings of the key input variables, what kind of variability still exists in the performance measures? How do you know? Show me the data.

(Continued on next page)

Table 4.6 Questions Leaders Need to Ask in the DMAIC Phases

Control

13. Have we implemented a process flow and control system to sustain the gains and continuously improve the process? Show me the data.

14. How much improvement has the value stream or process shown in the past six months? How much time and/or money have our efforts saved the company? Show me the data.

Table 4.6 Questions Leaders Need to Ask in the DMAIC Phases

Finally, Six Sigma also provides a set of tools that can be used in each of the five phases to help answer the questions. These tools are shown in Figure 4.16.

Define	Measure	Analyze	Improve	Control
Benchmarking	Confidence Intervals	Affinity Diagram	DFSS	Control Charts
FMEA	Measurement System Analysis	Brainstorming	DOE	Control Plan
IPO Diagram	Multi-Voting	Cause & Effect Diagram	Kanban	Reaction Plan
Kano's Model	Nominal Group Technique	e-test	Line Balancing	Run Charts
Knowledge Based Mgt	Pairwise Ranking	F-test	Mistake Proofing	Audits/Reports
Project Charter	Physical Process Flow	Fault Tree Analysis	PF/CE/CNX/SOP	
SIPOC Model	Process Capability Analysis	FMEA	Physical Space Relationship Chart	
Quality Function Deployment	Process Flow Diagram	Force Field Analysis	Single Minute Exchange of Dies	
Voice of Customer	Process Observation	Histogram	Standard Work	
	Time Value Map	Historical Data Analysis	Takt Time	
	Value Stream Mapping	Pareto Chart	Theory of Constraints	
	Waste Analysis	Reality Tree	Total Productive Maintenance	
		Regression Analysis	Visual Management	
		Scatter Diagram	Work Cell Design	
		t-test	5S Workplace Organization	
		Thematic Content Analysis		
		Tukey End Count Test		
		5 Whys		

Note: Tools May Be Used In Multiple Phases

Figure 4.16   Six Sigma Tools and Techniques to Answer Questions and Generate Knowledge

To deploy and implement a Six Sigma initiative requires building an infrastructure to support the methodology and the use of the tools and techniques to deliver results. Some of the key players in this infrastructure are Champions, Black Belts, Green Belts, and Master Black Belts.

The role of a Champion (or sponsor) includes identifying and defining key projects that can best benefit the organization. Champions also identify Black Belt and Green Belt candidates and align them with the projects. A Champion provides financial and organizational resources to train and equip Belts to accomplish project goals. Champions create and maintain project momentum. They break down barriers to project completion and push the projects across the finish line. Their most enviable tasks are to recognize and reward success and propagate success stories to generate cultural change. Champions receive approximately 3 days of training in Six Sigma implementation strategy and tools.

Black Belts and Green Belts are project executioners who adhere to the DMAIC methodology, applying the tools as needed to acquire the appropriate knowledge. They are the experts at using the tools and getting a Six Sigma project team to work together. They take charge in areas of needed improvement identified by their Champion. Belts are change agents who challenge old ways of doing business for the purpose of gaining breakthrough improvements. Black Belts receive double the amount of training (approximately 4 weeks spread over 4 months) that a Green Belt receives (about 2 weeks spread over 2 months). Thus, Black Belts are usually assigned the more strategic projects and are recommended to be full-time on their projects. Green Belt projects are lesser in scope and are more localized. Green Belts work on their project on a part-time basis and can assist Black Belts on their projects, thereby leveraging the capability of a Black Belt to multi-task on several projects simultaneously.

Master Black Belts are the chosen few (approximately 1 in 10) of the Black Belts who go on to further training (like Train-the-Trainer) so that they can become the internal trainers and coaches for other Belts coming up through the ranks. If an organization wants to become self-sustaining in the application of Six Sigma, Master Black Belts are the primary vehicle for doing so. Master Black Belts also serve on the Leadership Team or Steering Committee that is responsible for rolling out the deployment and implementation of Six Sigma in an organization. While Champions serve as the business mentors for Belts, Master Black Belts are the technical mentors for the Belts.

Besides the infrastructure needed to deploy and implement Six Sigma, there are three major phases that an organization goes through during the deployment process. These three phases, which are called Initialization, Execution, and Assessment, are shown in Figure 4.17 with the corresponding activities that are associated with each phase. As one can see, Six Sigma formalizes many of the concepts that have already been addressed in this text.

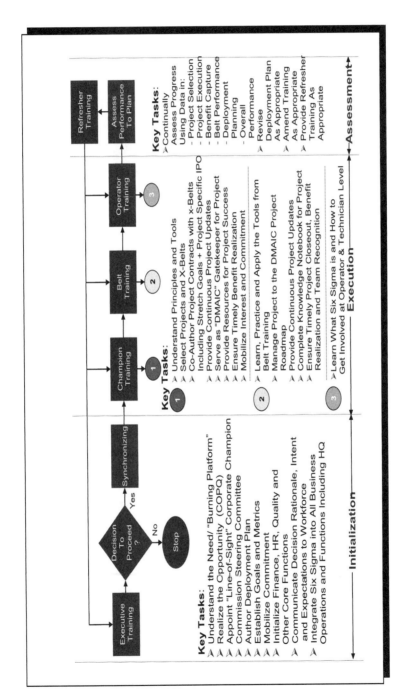

Figure 4.17 Rolling Out Six Sigma: The Big Picture

To summarize the critical factors that an organization needs to control in order to maximize the business impact of Six Sigma, we use a dual-IPO diagram to describe the key inputs and outputs for a successful implementation and realization of Six Sigma. These are shown in Figure 4.18. Analogous to the IPO diagrams we have used previously to indicate the key factors we need to control in a process, if an organization successfully controls the 10 critical input variables shown in Figure 4.18, it is almost guaranteed to have a successful Six Sigma deployment.

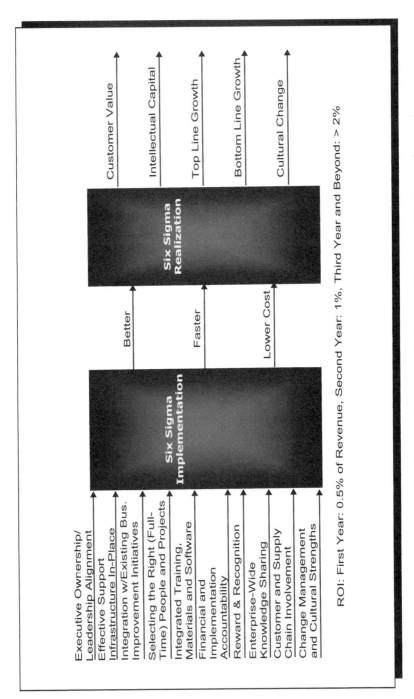

Figure 4.18 Critical Success Factors to Maximize Business Impact

This concludes our introductory treatment of Six Sigma and the DMAIC methodology. It should be clear that Six Sigma/DMAIC provides an improvement strategy that combines the power of being able to answer the knowledge generating questions with the infrastructure, rollout, and critical success factors that have made Six Sigma the strategy of choice for many organizations. More details will be presented in subsequent chapters when the evolution of Six Sigma will be shown to take on an even broader meaning and capability.

Chapter 5

LEAN SIX SIGMA

"An investment in knowledge always pays the best interest."

Benjamin Franklin

It is widely recognized in today's marketplace that the two leading improvement strategies are "Lean" and "Six Sigma." There is much evidence to indicate that both strategies have contributed substantially to bottom line results, improved value delivery to customers, and enhanced competitiveness. Noting the power and uniqueness of each strategy, practitioners have begun applying both approaches as needed to generate results for their organizations. Not surprisingly terms such as "Lean Sigma" or "Lean Six Sigma" have emerged. In helping our customers apply the principles and tools of Lean and Six Sigma, we have seen the need to use them as a dynamic, synergistic force, rather than what is often perceived as two competing strategies. The purpose of this chapter is to first define Lean and Six Sigma in as much detail as is needed to give the reader a good feel for what each is about. Then we will address the natural synergy of the two by showing how they complement one another, thus arriving at what is now most often called Lean Six Sigma, an improvement strategy that harnesses the best of both worlds. Please see Figure 5.1

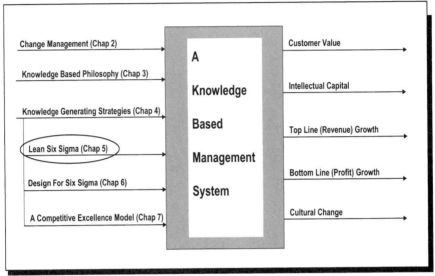

Figure 5.1 KBM IPO Diagram

Definition of Lean

Lean is the continuous elimination of unnecessary, non-value added steps within a process. It espouses two primary principles to which all of the Lean tools contribute: flow and pull. The principle of flow dates back to the Ford Motor Company in the early twentieth century when Henry Ford introduced the assembly line process to mass produce the Model T. The restocking system in a supermarket is a good example of the principle of pull. Toyota was no doubt one of the first companies to successfully combine these two concepts, and today its Toyota Production System (TPS) is the flag bearer of what is now commonly called Lean. It is interesting to note that Toyota does not use the term "Lean." That term was coined by James Womack at MIT who has authored the texts *The Machine That Changed the World: The*

Story of Lean Production and *Lean Thinking*. The concepts of value, making value flow uninterrupted at the pull of the customer, single piece versus batch flow, and the elimination of all activities that do not contribute value to the customer serve as the foundation of Lean.

At the most basic level, Lean is about speed. And since speed is about rates which necessarily use time in their calculations, Lean is about time. Lean essentially searches out and destroys wasted time. It also searches out and destroys wasted materials, as well as wasted effort. In essence, Lean is a waste eliminator, whether that waste be in terms of time, material, or effort. An amazing fact is that when we eliminate wasted time, materials, and effort, the quality of our products and services will get better and the cost will go down. This is not intuitive by any means, but as we progress through this chapter, this point should become clearer. Henry Ford understood this relationship well. He considered inventory as material waste and time waste as an even greater evil, because time waste is 100% unrecoverable. Then where did Ford go wrong, if his processes were so "lean?" Recalling that Ford once said, "you (customer) can have any color of this automobile that you want, as long as it is black," maybe the voice of the customer was not altogether clear back then either.

Specifically, what is the definition of a "lean" process or activity? One of the most important metrics of Lean is the ratio of value added time to total processing time. This is sometimes called Process Cycle Efficiency. In other words,

Process Cycle Efficiency = Value Added Time/Total Processing Time,

where Value Added Time is defined as the work time a customer would consider necessary to create the product or service. Surprisingly, most process cycle efficiencies, when measured in percentages, do not exceed 5%. That may be hard to believe, but it is true and it can be verified by observing processes and taking the measurements. In most applications, be they manufacturing or transactional, a process is considered "lean" if the process cycle efficiency is at least 25%.

A relatively unknown relationship that explains quite a bit about rates, time, and implied cost is given by Little's Law, which is shown in Table 5.1. This relationship does make sense. For example, if I enter a queue to exit an airport parking lot and I see 20 cars ahead of me in the only check-out lane that is open and if I also notice that the bar or gate is raised once every minute to allow a car to exit, I can easily estimate my cycle time as 20 minutes. In this case, WIP is 20 (cars) and the TH is 1 (car/minute). Although cost is not readily apparent in this relationship, cost enters the equation through WIP. Slow

Cycle Time (CT):	The time from when a job is released into a routing to when it exits, e.g., time from"order entry" to "ship" -- includes move time, queue time, setup time, and process time; the time a product spends as WIP; also known as lead time
Throughput (TH):	Quanity of good product produced in a process per unit time
Work in Process (WIP):	Inventory between the start and end points of a product routing
Little's Law:	$$CT = \frac{WIP}{TH}$$

Table 5.1 Little's Law: Capacity Analysis Terms and Relationships

processes (i.e., large cycle times) are almost always associated with large amounts of WIP, which generates hidden costs such as rework, scrap, overhead, and invested capital. By reducing CT, WIP is also reduced, and thus cost reductions are also realized. Lean considers inventory as WIP, hardly the "asset" we considered it to be in our accounting classes. Little's Law also provides project champions or sponsors some insight into expected cycle times for executing projects in a Lean Six Sigma rollout. If champions continue to place more and more projects on the plates of a fixed number of Belts, i.e., increase the WIP, we can expect projects to take much longer to be completed. One last note of caution is in order for Little's Law, and that is the relationship holds for "average" values of CT, WIP, and TH. This extends to the whole concept of Lean as well, as almost all measurements taken in a strictly Lean context do not address variation in cycle time, throughput, and other measurements that may be taken. Fortunately, this shortcoming is alleviated by integrating the concept of Six Sigma with Lean.

Definition of Six Sigma

As its name implies, Six Sigma has statistical connotations. Notwithstanding our treatment of Six Sigma and the DMAIC methodology in Chapter 4, there are some basic definitions that anyone who plans to be associated with Lean Six Sigma needs to know. For example, what is a sigma? Why is it "six?" Personally, this author likes "seven" better, and it also starts with the letter "s" giving us almost the same alliterative effect. Fortunately for all, there are some basic definitions that we cannot alter or change based on our feelings. We begin with the definition of a sigma.

The lower case Greek letter sigma, **σ**, represents the **standard deviation** of a set of data. Standard deviation is a measure of variability inherent in the data. There are other useful measures we use in Lean Six Sigma to describe a data set, such as the mean or average, which represents the center or balance point of a data set. However, we cannot do a Lean Six Sigma project without collecting data and furthermore, we cannot do a Lean Six Sigma project without talking about sigma. This awareness needs to be firmly implanted in the reader's mind now. While the mathematical equation definition of sigma is beyond the scope of this text (besides, the standard deviation of any data set is easily obtained by the click of a mouse button and easy-to-use software), the graphical meaning is easy and that is what is presented here. While we are at it, we will also define the mean in graphical terms, too.

Suppose we have collected a set of data points or values in the Measure phase of DMAIC in a Lean Six Sigma project for some CTC or performance measure like cycle time. The individual circles in Figure 5.2 represent these data points, each of which represents a particular cycle time observation. That is, y represents cycle time. It appears that there are well over 100 data points shown in this figure. The clustering of the data points appears to follow the famous bell shaped curve or normal distribution which is superimposed on top of the data points. The mean value or average value shown in the figure is the balance point of the distribution. This is where we would have to place a fulcrum if we were to balance this data set horizontally. Visual inspection allows us to approximate this value at about 153, so $\bar{y} \approx 153$. Graphically, the value of σ can also be easily obtained by locating a point of inflection on the normal curve. A point of inflection is where the two types of curvature (concave up and concave down) meet. There are two such points on the normal curve, as shown in Figure 5.2. The value of sigma can be estimated by estimating the length of the horizontal line segment from a point of inflection to the center line. Since the rightmost point of inflection appears to be directly over 160 and the mean is 153, it appears that σ ≈ 7.

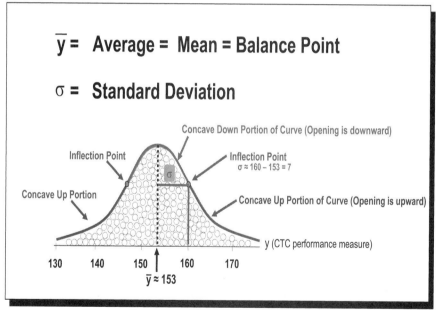

Figure 5.2 Graphical Meaning of $\bar{y}$ and σ

Knowing the graphical meaning of $\bar{y}$ and σ makes it easy to understand the definition of "sigma level" or "sigma capability." The smaller the value of σ, the greater the "σ capability." This may not seem intuitive until one realizes that "σ capability" (like a 4σ or 5σ capability) is defined in terms of how many "σ's" can be absorbed within a specified tolerance range of the performance measure. Thus, smaller values of σ allow more σ's to be squeezed within a specified tolerance range and hence the greater the σ capability. This definition is presented and graphically displayed in Figure 5.3, where two normal distributions are shown centered between a lower and upper specification limit.

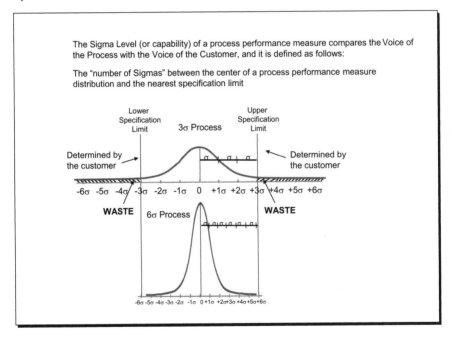

Figure 5.3 Graphical Meaning of Sigma Level (or capability)

The specification limits represent the Voice of the Customer, and the data distributions (normal curves) represent the Voice of the Process. Based on the definition, the upper curve represents a 3σ process while the lower curve represents a 6σ process. This is because the value of σ is smaller in the lower curve than it is in the upper curve, and consequently more line segments of length σ can be squeezed between the center of the distribution and the nearest specification in the lower curve than in the upper curve. Clearly, σ is the "shape" parameter of a data distribution. Considering the fact that the percentages of area under the curve are as shown in Figure 5.4, no matter what the shape of the curve, a 6σ process will have a much greater percentage of its data within specification than a 3σ process will. That is why the 6σ process shown in Figure 5.3 is a better process than the 3σ process. There is less waste (shaded area under the curve that is outside of specification) in the 6σ process than there is in the 3σ process.

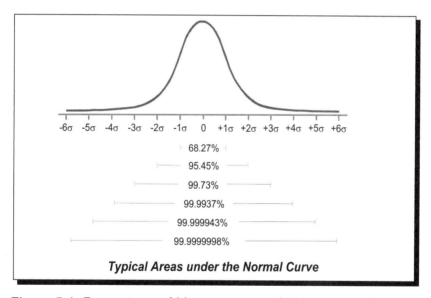

Figure 5.4 Percentage of Measurements Within Various Sigma
Intervals of a Normal Distribution

The preceding definitions conveniently use the normal distribution or bell shaped curve, which is the most common distribution for continuous data, i.e., data collected on a continuous scale. Defect rates for continuous measurements like this are equivalent to the proportion of measurements (or area under the curve) that fall outside of the specification limits. Recall that this is represented by the shaded areas shown in Figure 5.3. But there are many other distributions, including binomial distributions in which each data element is considered defective or non-defective, good or bad, acceptable or unacceptable, etc. In cases like this, the capability measure of choice is dpmo (defects per million opportunities). The good news is that all of the capability measures that one might use are correlated as shown in Table 5.2. This table shows the correlation between 3 different capability measures. A 6σ capability is synonymous with 3.4 dpmo, a 5σ capability means 233 dpmo , a 4σ capability has 6,210 dpmo, etc. Inherent in the use of any dpmo measure is the fact that the meaning of an "opportunity" and a "defect" must be clear and very well defined.

σ Capability	DPMO*	RTY*
2	308,537	69.1%
3	66,807	93.3%
4	6,210	99.4%
5	233	99.97%
6	3.4	99.99966%
Process Capability	Defects per Million Opportunities	Rolled Throughput Yield

Six Sigma is a standard of Excellence.
It means less than 4 Defects per Million Opportunities.

* assumes 1.5 sigma shift in average

Table 5.2 Relationship Between Various Capability Measures

You have now conquered the basic definitions of Six Sigma. However, Lean Six Sigma is much more than a mathematical definition, as the next sections will illustrate.

The Synergy of Lean and Six Sigma

Lean and Six Sigma are complementary in nature and, if done properly, represent a long-term business improvement strategy that can produce unprecedented results. While Lean focuses on eliminating non-value added steps and activities in a process, Six Sigma focuses on reducing variation from the remaining value added steps. Lean makes sure we are working on the right activities, and Six Sigma makes sure we are doing the right things right the very first time we do them. Doing the wrong things (i.e., performing non-value added activities) is pure waste. And worse yet, the investment we make in becoming proficient at doing the wrong things right the very first time we do them is also total waste. Lean and Six Sigma mean simplify and perfect. Perfecting non-value added steps in a process is useless and wasteful. Lean defines and establishes the value flow as pulled by the customer, and Six Sigma makes the value flow smoothly without interruption. We need both of them, and Figure 5.5 illustrates this synergistic concept. Another way of looking at the synergy of Lean and Six Sigma is that Lean removes the non-value added activities, and Six Sigma pours value back into the process by removing variation from critical value added steps. This is also apparent in Figure 5.5.

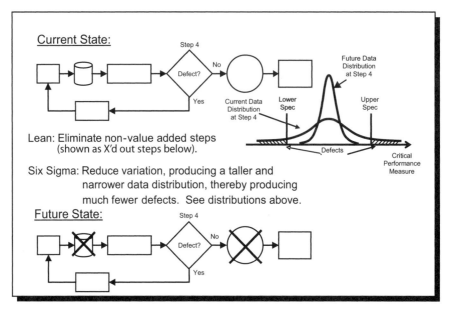

Figure 5.5 The Synergy of Lean and Six Slgma

The relationship between Lean and Six Sigma can be even more emphatically demonstrated using a chart that was developed by the Six Sigma Research Institute at Motorola. Table 5.3 shows the essence of a chart Bill Smith showed Bob Galvin, then the CEO of Motorola, in 1986 when Motorola was desperately trying to gain a competitive position in the electronics marketplace. Using this chart, Bill Smith, now deceased and who some consider the Father of Six Sigma, was able to convince his boss that Six Sigma was the key to their future.   Perhaps unknown to Smith at the time, he was also implicating Lean. We have found this chart to be the "breakthrough" message for many leaders throughout the world in their quest to understand what Lean Six Sigma is all about.

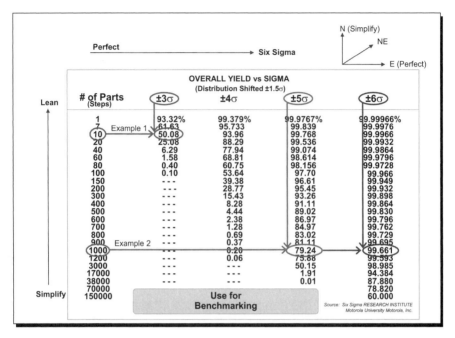

Table 5.3 Relationship Between Lean and Six Sigma

The percentages in the body of the chart represent Rolled Throughput Yield (RTY) for a given number of steps (or parts), shown in the left column, and a corresponding Sigma Level, shown across the top. Only the 3, 4, 5, and 6 sigma columns are shown, as are selected levels of "complexity" in the leftmost column. The first example shown on the chart is if we have a relatively simple 10-step process and each step is rated as a 3σ step, then the resulting RTY will be an abysmal 50.08%. This means that approximately half the starts will make it through the entire 10-step process unscathed, while the other half will encounter problems at some point or points along the way, causing potential rework, scrap, and waste, thereby fueling this "hidden factory" of waste and cost of poor quality.

Fully aware that processes can be much more complicated than that, suppose we assume a second scenario, namely a 1,000-step process with each step being rated as a 5σ step. Such a process is not uncommon when considering a circuit board where each solder joint can be considered a step. The corresponding RTY for this second example is a meager 79.24%, a resulting board yield that would not allow a company like Motorola to be competitive in the marketplace, according to Galvin. Thus, Bill Smith steered Bob Galvin to the next column to the right, the 6σ column. For the same 1,000-step process, the RTY becomes an amazing 99.66% RTY, clearly a competitive percentage. Now you know the "rest of the story," namely why it is called Six Sigma. That being the history lesson, there is much more on this chart still to be digested.

A quick survey of the chart clearly shows the highest RTYs to be in the upper right of the chart. Thus, it behooves us to have an approach to get to the upper right of the chart, or in navigator terms, move to the Northeast part of this map. On a map, how does one move toward the Northeast? Not a trick question, the answer is simply go North and go East. To the authors, going North means Simplify. In the marketplace today, it is called Lean. That is, remove non-value added steps and reduce complexity, or simplify. To us, going East means Perfect (verb form: per fect´). The marketplace calls it Six Sigma. That is, reduce variation in the critical value added steps, or perfect those steps. Like a true journey, the Lean Six Sigma journey requires alternating movements to the north and to the east, with the ultimate goal of highly competitive RTYs.

If an organization does not have a disciplined, repeatable improvement strategy like Lean Six Sigma that will take them to the northeast part of this chart, the movement will typically be in a southerly direction, because as soon as we encounter problems, the natural tendency is to add steps. Granted, at times we do have to add steps in order to plug the leak in the dike, so to speak, but unfortunately more often than not those steps we put in 10 years ago are still there today and are completely non-value added. That is why we need something like Lean Six Sigma to ferret out the waste and perfect the good. One last point about Table 5.3: the numbers don't lie. Today or 100 years from now, whenever we take .999767 and raise it to the 1,000th power, we will always get .792, whether we call it Lean Six Sigma or not. Yes, Lean Six Sigma is a label, and even if that name should go away over time, the numbers in the chart will not go away. Despite the rigor in this section, it is hoped that the reader now has a good grasp of the synergistic nature of Lean and Six Sigma, which hereafter we shall call Lean Six Sigma. We conclude this section with the five basic operating principles of Lean Six Sigma, which are shown in Table 5.4.

1.	Specify value in the eyes of the customer.
2.	Identify the value stream and eliminate waste/variation.
3.	Make value flow smoothly at the pull of the customer.
4.	Involve, align and empower employees.
5.	Continuously improve knowledge in pursuit of perfection.

Table 5.4 Lean Six Sigma Principles

Deployment and Implementation Issues

Having already discussed the first three principles of Lean Six Sigma in some detail, we devote the remainder of this chapter to the last two principles, namely empowering our employees and continuously improving knowledge. The major deployment and implementation issues are directly related to people, projects, and prioritization, so that is what our discussion will focus on.

One of the critical differences between Lean Six Sigma and other improvement strategies is the infrastructure that needs to be established in an organization to make it happen. We have already addressed this topic briefly in Chapter 4. While everyone in an organization needs to play a part in making Lean Six Sigma successful, there are some critical players that form the backbone of a Lean Six Sigma rollout. These are Champions, Black Belts, Green Belts, and Master Black Belts. These terms or names are fairly standard throughout industry, but the reader must be warned that variability takes its toll here, too, in terms of competency. We have summarized the roles, profiles, and training of these key players in Table 5.5 to make it easier for the reader to compare and contrast these aspects for the different players.

	CHAMPION (Mentor)	BLACK BELT (Expert)	GREEN BELT (Specialist)	MASTER BLACK BELT (Master)
PROFILE	• senior leader or manager • respected leader and mentor of business issues • strong proponent of Lean Six Sigma who asks the right questions • serves as a business mentor for Belts	• respected by peers and management • master of basic and advanced tools • able to turn data into information	• respected by peers • proficient in basic and advanced tools • able to turn data into information	• technically excellent in the knowledge and application of lean & statistical tools • excellent communicator • respected Lean Six Sigma role model at all levels of the company
ROLE	• identify projects and align Belts with the projects • provide financial and or-ganizational resources to accomplish project goals • create & maintain project momentum • break down barriers and push projects across the finish line	• leads strategic, high impact process improvement projects • change agent • teaches and mentors cross-functional team members & Green Belts • full-time project leader • converts gains into $	• leads important process improve-ment teams • leads, trains and coaches on tools and analysis • assists Black Belts • typically part-time on a project	• technical mentor for Black Belts and Green Belts • internal consultant and trainer • generates breakthrough thinking for improving Lean Six Sigma process • may serve on Lean Six Sigma Leadership Team
TRAINING	• 3 days of Champion training • need to know tools and deployment and imple-mentation strategy	• four or five 1-week sessions with one month in between to apply project review in every session	• two 1-week sessions with one month in between to apply • project review in 2nd session	• 1-2 weeks (including Train-the-Trainer) beyond Black Belt training
NUMBERS	• enough to gain critical mass (15-30 %)	• 1 per 50 to 100 employees (1 - 2 %)	• 1 per 20 employees (5%)	• approximately 10% of the number of Black Belts

Table 5.5 Comparison of Roles

The numbers shown are recommendations only. Each organization must decide what is best for them in terms of numbers. The percentages shown for the Belts are for those who are **actively** working on projects. For example, a Black Belt may work on projects full-time for a period of 18-24 months. After his or her tenure as an active Black Belt, he or she will move to some other position in the organization, continuing to apply the tools and methodology but not necessarily being active in formal project execution. An organization needs a self-sufficiency plan in place to continually replenish the active Black Belt cadre. This is where the capability of a Master Black Belt can really help. Bringing more and more people up through the ranks and providing them the Black Belt and Green Belt capabilities sustains the effort and ultimately changes the culture. The long-term goal for any Lean Six Sigma initiative should be to transform it from a project-based initiative into a culture-based initiative. But without the disciplined, repeatable execution of projects over a sustainable period of time, the culture change will not happen. Habits must be ingrained into the hearts, minds, and souls of individuals in order to make performance improvement stick as part of the culture. There is a reason the martial arts terminology is used in Lean Six Sigma. It exemplifies discipline, repeatability, and the mental toughness to break through any barrier.

Regarding Champions, there are different types of Champions. Deployment Champions are responsible for the overall deployment and rollout of Lean Six Sigma in an organization. These are typically full-time positions reporting directly to the highest position in the organization. Then there are project champions, also called sponsors or process owners, who are responsible for specific projects they have identified and to which they assign Belts. These project champions or sponsors are key individuals, because they work directly with the Belts to push the projects across the finish line. They are responsible and accountable for successful project completion. Belts move on to other projects, but the project champion/sponsor/owner must live with the change induced by the project and sustain the improved process going forward even after the project is completed.

Regarding education and training, Figure 5.6 gives a pictorial representation of the length and depth of education for the various players. Note that the first two weeks of Black Belt training constitute Green Belt training. Thus, Green Belts and Black Belts could be trained together for the first two weeks, thus saving training budget. Also, those Green Belts who have done several projects and want to move on to become Black Belts could pick up the remainder of a Black Belt curriculum by completing the last two weeks without having to redo the first two weeks. Similarly, a Black Belt who goes on to become an organization's Master Black Belt extends his or her education by a certain number of days. One thing must be made clear: just because someone goes through the Belt training does not make that person a certified Black Belt or Green Belt. At the time of their training, they are really Belt "candidates" even though we may be referring to them as Black Belts or Green Belts during their training regimen. One is not a true Belt unless one is certified. There is no single body for certifying Belts in Lean Six Sigma. However, any reputable certification criteria must include the following:

1. Successful completion of a legitimate training program

2. Successful completion of a written examination which covers the training

3. Successful completion of a project or projects

4. Successfully documenting the project in written format

5. Successfully briefing the project to the organization's leadership

We not only want the Belts to become knowledgeable about the tools and methodology of Lean Six Sigma and deliver financial results via the projects, but we want them to use this opportunity to improve their communications ability as well. Items 4 and 5 target this goal.

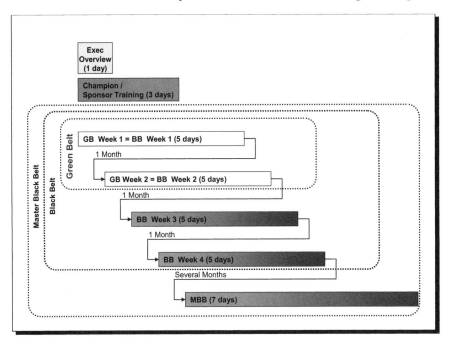

Figure 5.6 Relative Depth of Education in Lean Six Sigma

The empowerment of employees necessarily includes equipping them with the latest in the tools and methodology which are used to execute projects. Lean Six Sigma also uses the DMAIC methodology but with an expanded set of tools over that which was shown in Figure 4.16 – the Six Sigma tools and techniques. The new expanded set of tools appears in Figure 5.7. Note that the added tools are in italics.

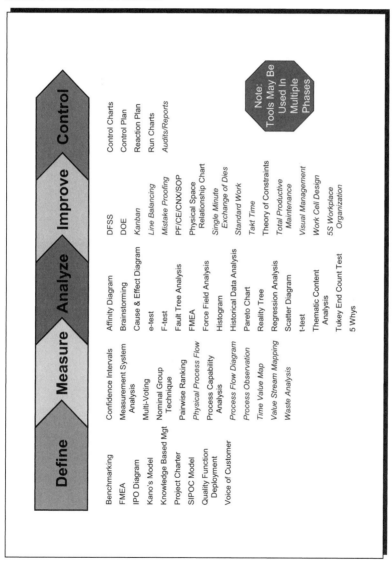

Figure 5.7 Lean Six Sigma Tools and Techniques

Finally, with regard to people, what characterizes a successful Black Belt? And are there criteria we can use to select them? We consider the group of Black Belts, because Black Belts comprise the largest group of full-time Lean Six Sigma practitioners. First and foremost, do not select a person to become a Black Belt candidate if he or she does not want to do it. This is too great an opportunity for someone who really wants to become a Black Belt to expend a slot on someone who doesn't. Our experience indicates there are some key characteristics of Black Belts that should be taken into consideration as part of an organization's selection criteria. These include:

- Proven performer

- Loyal to the organization

- Knowledgeable of the processes to be improved

- Problem solver who is attentive to detail

- Analytical and not afraid to learn new tools and techniques

- Team builder

- Leadership qualities

The last two criteria listed are crucial, because we have yet to see any Black Belt training substantially change someone's personality. In today's learning environment, the education and training can provide any motivated individual with the appropriate skills in the tools and techniques. But the people skills are not as easily obtained. The old adage still applies: "the hard stuff is easy, but the soft stuff is hard." Being selected as a Black Belt candidate should be considered a huge opportunity, as well as an honor, because the skills and experience that will be absorbed will make this person a much better person in all aspects of life. In short, it will make them better decision makers. As my mother once said, "better yourself or you're going to stay that way!"

The last operating principle of Lean Six Sigma, to continuously improve knowledge in pursuit of perfection, requires project execution. Project selection has sometimes been called the "Achilles heel" of Lean Six Sigma. Leadership and management are responsible for selecting the projects that the Belts will be working. It is only a reflection on themselves when after the fact they say, "we did not get the benefits because we did not select the projects well." While project scoping can be dicey at times, the mining of projects should not be difficult. Most organizations have potential project opportunities that are more numerous than can possibly be worked with the resources they have. Yet, we find that most Lean Six Sigma Champions struggle in this area, and that is why we devote the remainder of this chapter to project selection and benefit realization.

We have found three primary areas that are usually ripe for mining projects. We categorize these areas as Burning Issues, Cost of Poor Quality and Waste, and Strategic Linkage. Burning issues can be broken down further into the more tangible areas shown in Table 5.6. If an organization has none of these issues, then it either doesn't need Lean Six Sigma or its leadership and management are oblivious to what is going on in their company. The Cost of Poor Quality and Waste have been defined previously in Table 4.4. Recall that they include internal failure costs, external failure costs, appraisal costs, prevention costs, and lost opportunity costs. Strategic linkage refers to those areas that are tied to the strategically driven business measures shown in Table 5.7.

- Customer demands/complaints

    - Delivery times are too slow

    - Costs are too high

    - Too many failures in products and services

- Needing to respond to competitor gains

- "Urgent" business needs

    - Expenses are too high

    - Erosion of customer base

- Shareholder requirements

    - Quarterly goals, end-of-year goals, etc.

- Excessive warranty costs

- Community/societal interests

- Management "intuition"

Table 5.6 Burning Issues

• Customer retention rate
• Overall product/service yield rates
• Customer satisfaction rate
• Product market share
• Revenue
• Profit margin
• EBITDA (Earnings Before Interest, Taxes, Depreciation, and Amortization)
• Employee turnover
• "Operational Excellence"
• Capacity
• Growth
• Expenses

Table 5.7 Strategically Driven Business Measures

A Lean Six Sigma project addresses issues or problems for which the answer or solution is unknown. That is precisely why we use the DMAIC methodology, which provides the format and tools for finding the best solutions. If we already know the answer to the problem or know how to correct an issue, then that is a Just-Do-It or JDI project, not a Lean Six Sigma project.   Unfortunately, many times we think we know the solution to an issue, but we really don't. Thus, even if we think we know the answer to a problem, it still may be advisable to go through the DMAIC process without a predisposition to a solution in order to see what the methodology tells us about the solution.

> **"It's what we know that ain't so that can kill us."**
>
> *Will Rogers*

A simple-to-use checklist of questions can be used to help ascertain if a potential project fits the mold of a Lean Six Sigma project. These questions are as follows:

1. Does this project contribute to delivering greater value to our customers?

2. Does this project build intellectual capital for our business?

3. Does this project contribute to the bottom line, i.e., profit margin?

4. Does this project contribute to improved revenue?

5. Does this project contribute to cultural improvement for our organization?

Every Lean Six Sigma project should contribute directly or indirectly to at least one of these five areas. Furthermore, the projects should be scoped so that a project does not take longer than 6 months to complete. If a project drags on beyond the 6-month mark, it is highly likely to die on the vine because leadership and management will lose interest and the momentum for project completion will wane. It is critical to get quick hitting successes out of the gate with a Belt's first project. Success is the best indicator for future successes, and early project successes will help develop support and momentum within an organization for the rollout of Lean Six Sigma.

Once a project is mined and nominated via a project charter, it enters a hopper or repository of projects awaiting execution. For most organizations, there will be more projects awaiting execution than there are resources (Champions and Belts) to execute them. Hence, some sort of prioritization mechanism must be applied to the projects to determine which ones should be accomplished first. Lean Six Sigma provides many prioritization tools that can be used, like Pairwise Ranking, a Pugh Decision Matrix, or a Multi-Voting technique.   We present the following Benefit/Effort Graph that illustrates a simple but yet very powerful technique to prioritize projects. It is shown in Figure 5.8.

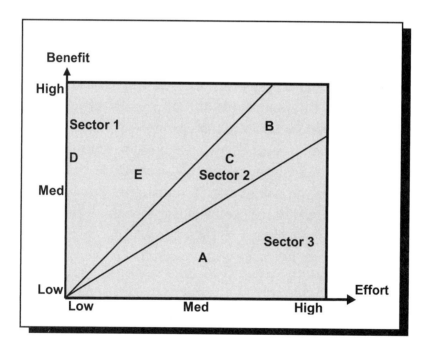

Figure 5.8 Benefit/Effort Graph

To use this graph, we plot or place each project in the 2 - dimensional grid based on the benefit and the effort required to generate that benefit. This can be done in a group setting. Suppose projects A,B,C,D, and E have been placed in the grid as shown in Figure 5.8. The projects in Sector 1 are the most desirable projects, followed by those in Sector 2. The projects in Sector 3 are the least desirable. Thus, a legitimate prioritization for the 5 projects shown in Figure 5.8 might be: D,E,C,B,A.

Not all Lean Six Sigma efforts will require a full-blown DMAIC application in order to achieve quick hitting results. There is a category of effort called Rapid Improvement Events (RIEs). RIEs can be accomplished under a variety of formats. One of the most common is called a Kaizen event. "Kaizen," a Japanese word that means "continuous improvement," is an intense effort by a cross-functional team that is assembled to produce very rapid results in a 3-5 day period. Kaizen events are often used within the DMAIC cycle to supplement or enhance a larger ongoing project. Since they are "improvement" events, they are particularly valuable in the Improve phase of a DMAIC project. Kaizen efforts that are stand-alone events run the risk of having the targeted process or value stream, after showing considerable improvement, revert back to its old state after a few weeks or months, because the controls (the "C" in DMAIC) were not adequately implemented. Following the DMAIC methodology and imbedding such RIEs within it will remedy that situation. All Lean Six Sigma DMAIC projects will necessarily involve the collection of data. By definition, if there is no data involved in a project or an event, it cannot be a Lean Six Sigma project or event.

We conclude this chapter with some remarks about benefit realization from Lean Six Sigma projects. Financial results must always be independently validated by a financial analyst. The Champions and Belts do not validate the savings from their projects. The savings are computed at the end of the project, looking at, for example, the COPQ after the project versus the COPQ before the project. If the project generates recurring savings—and many will, the maximum benefit period that is counted is for 12 months (to get the annualized benefits). Financial tracking rules must be established prior to the start of the project. For example, do we count hard savings only, or are soft savings (cost avoidance) also going to be credited? Focus should always be on hard P&L savings. However, if we focus solely on hard savings, many excellent projects will be overlooked, especially with regard to the Voice of the Customer. Additionally, there will typically be push back from business units because all projects will be viewed as cost reduction efforts. On the other hand, soft savings can be difficult to measure in terms of dollars/yen/euro, etc.

Our recommendation is to ensure that all projects are linked to the fulfillment of key business measures like on-time delivery, top-line growth, reduction in customer complaints, reduced lead times, improved invoice accuracy, etc., to which accountability is linked. When doing Lean Six Sigma project reviews at standing management meetings, report on both hard ($$) savings and soft (non $$) savings and offer credit to both.

This concludes our overview of Lean Six Sigma, which was designed to give the reader a perspective of the key concepts that make it one of the most powerful improvement strategies used today. More detail on the tools and techniques of Lean Six Sigma, as well as examples of their usage, can be obtained from the texts described in the introductory pages of this text, as well as from those in the References section.

Chapter 6

DESIGN FOR SIX SIGMA

"The systems and products that deliver value to our customers are perfectly designed to achieve the results we are getting today."

Anonymous

After reading the quote above, would you consider that statement to be true or false? Perfectly designed? No way, because nothing is ever **perfectly** designed. Perfectly designed to get the results we are getting today? Perhaps. There is much truth in that statement, especially if one considers the contrapositive, or logical equivalent, which says: "if we are not getting the results that we desire, then the designs that are delivering value are probably not perfect." The latter statement is more likely a better descriptor of the truth. The purpose of this chapter is to introduce the reader to the next evolutionary step beyond Lean Six Sigma (LSS). The title of this chapter could also have been labeled Design for Lean Six Sigma (DFLSS), which some of our clients call it. We have elected to call it Design for Six Sigma (DFSS) to place the emphasis on the fact that we are designing our products and services to achieve high capability in whatever performance measures may be required, including those in all three categories of quality, cost, and delivery. Clearly, LSS can be applied to any process, including the product development process, to reduce waste and variation in the process, in order to speed products to market and reduce cost. Though the product development process is certainly included in the scope of DFSS, it is not the emphasis here, because the LSS DMAIC methodology described in Chapter 5 is usually sufficient to improve that, although DFSS techniques may be needed to design or redesign that process, too. Instead, we are emphasizing the design characteristics of the products and services themselves in order to achieve high capability performance ratings. In and of itself, DFSS is a knowledge generating strategy. (See Figure 6.1). Its purpose is to generate knowledge much earlier in the life cycle of a product or service. That point will become clearer as we move through this chapter.

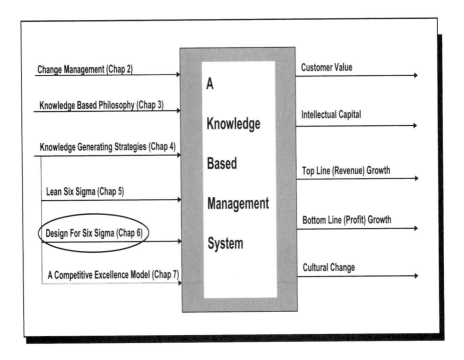

Figure 6.1 KBM IPO Diagram

Neither LSS nor DFSS just showed up on the radar screen yesterday. There has been a long history leading up to the onset of these two knowledge generating strategies, as shown in the Reality Tree in Figure 6.2. In fact, this text has already discussed some of the entries in this evolutionary trail.

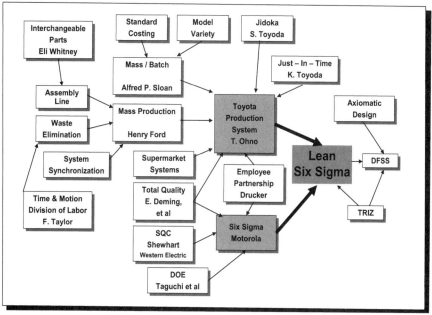

Figure 6.2 Performance Improvement Evolution

The Motivation for DFSS

Most organizations that start a DFSS initiative do so only after having deployed and experienced LSS for a couple of years. There is an important reason for that, and it is shown in Figure 6.3. Almost every Champion and Belt has experienced the curve in this graph. That is, after improving a process using DMAIC, the sigma capability or rating of key performance measures is usually not close to 6.

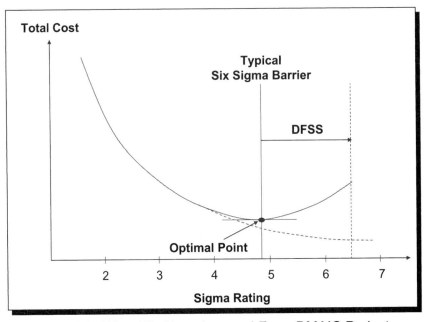

Figure 6.3 What We Have Learned From DMAIC Projects

The optimal point shown in this Total Cost curve is at a sigma rating of approximately 4.8. That is not to say that 4.8 is not a good sigma rating, because taking a 2σ process and using DMAIC to bring it to a 3σ or 4σ rating represents huge savings. The point of the graph is that DMAIC projects rarely, if ever, produce capability ratings greater than 5. Over the years, this has become known as the Six Sigma Barrier, and it usually occurs somewhere between 4 and 5. What that means is that there is no incentive to go beyond the barrier, because it will cost us more than the benefit we will receive. We would like the cost curve to proceed downward, so that there is financial incentive to get to 6 or beyond. What DFSS means to most organizations who undertake it is to move the Six Sigma Barrier out to the right as depicted in the graph, so that the cost curve continues to move downward and there is financial incentive to move to the higher sigma ratings. DMAIC has produced phenomenal results, but there is a limit to how far it can take us. We must always take into consideration the voice of the customer, because ultimately it is the customer who determines what the sigma capability must be.

> *"We may be able to genetically engineer a 6σ goat, but if the marketplace is a rodeo, a 4σ horse may be just fine."*
>
> *Anonymous*

The reason that DMAIC is limited is because it is usually applied later in the life cycle of a product or service, i.e., during the production period. As Figure 6.4 shows, DFSS focuses its application much earlier in the life cycle of a product or service, namely in the design and development phases. The curve in Figure 6.4 is really even more exacerbated than it appears, because the vertical axis is an exponential scale, not a linear scale. That is, the cost of making a design change earlier in the life cycle of a product or service is much, much less than it is later in the life cycle. If you don't believe that statement, just ask Ford Motor Company or Firestone/Bridgestone about what it cost them to gain knowledge about their designs later in the life cycle of their product (tires). We want to gain knowledge when costs are lowest and design in high capability right from the start.

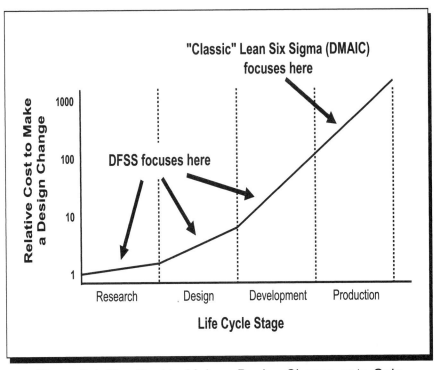

Figure 6.4 The Cost to Make a Design Change or to Gain Knowledge

The goals of DFSS are simple and straightforward:

1.   Reduce cycle time in the design and development process.

2.   Reduce the time to money (TTM).

3.   Reduce the cost of poor quality (COPQ).

4.   Improve the predictability of quality, cost, and delivery (QCD).

Dr. Norm Kuchar, formerly of General Electric Corporate R&D, who led GE's worldwide deployment of DFSS, stated in an interview in October of 2003 that

"Since GE began using DFSS on its new products, we have seen quality increases of at least +1σ at launch over previous designs. We have also seen a time to market decrease by at least 25% over previous launches and a cost savings of total resources utilized in the 20-40% range over the life cycle of a product."

A +1σ improvement in quality may not seem like much, but it is huge when one considers all of the performance measures that must be simultaneously improved for a given product. Dr. Kuchar's data correlates quite well with the industry standard graphs in Figure 6.5, which shows the ultimate benefits of DFSS. This figure compares the DFSS Vision with the Pre-DFSS Approach in three primary areas. The first area, total resources used, is the comparison of the two curves. The shaded area (Pre-DFSS) is much larger than the unshaded area under the curve (DFSS), meaning that the total resources used in a DFSS effort are much less than the Pre-DFSS. What is a sticking point is that the center of the DFSS distribution is much farther left than is the center of the Pre-DFSS distribution (the shaded area). That means in a DFSS initiative, resources must be allocated much sooner but overall, the total resources will be much less. Almost all companies would like to change the shaded double-humped curve into the curve on the left. It won't and cannot happen overnight, because companies don't have the available resources to do it. But it can happen one DFSS project or study at a time. Using a disciplined DFSS approach, organizations will be able to cut off the second hump of the shaded curve. That hump happens shortly after launch because of unanticipated problems cropping up in the field. We have all experienced that hump, either in the product or service industry, and know that it is not a pleasant ride.

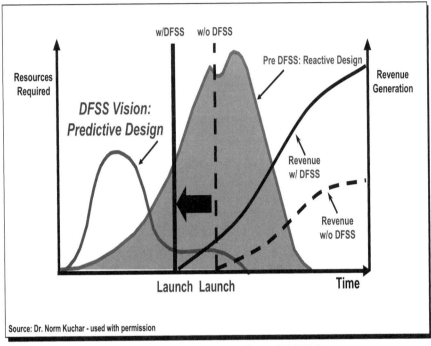

Figure 6.5 The Benefits of DFSS

A second comparison is with the two launch points. Clearly the DFSS launch point is earlier. That is, the time to money is much sooner. This has a synergistic or interaction effect with the revenue growth rate. Getting to market faster has multiple benefits. It creates greater market share, and it also allows a company to establish higher prices before the competition enters the market and is able to commoditize it. In summary, the Pre-DFSS approach means unhappy customers, unplanned resource drain, skyrocketing costs, and the likelihood of compromising the next product. For the DFSS Vision, problems are identified earlier when costs are lowest; there is faster market entry with earlier revenue stream and longer patent coverage; the total development costs are lower; and robust products at market entry mean delighted customers. Furthermore, resources are now available for the **next** game-changing product. The idea behind DFSS is that upfront investment is most effective and efficient, and it will show customers incredible value right from the start. DFSS and DMAIC can both help in the transition from the double-humped curve to the DFSS Vision curve.

DFSS should move a company from a reactive approach to design quality to a vision of predictive design quality, as depicted in Figure 6.6.

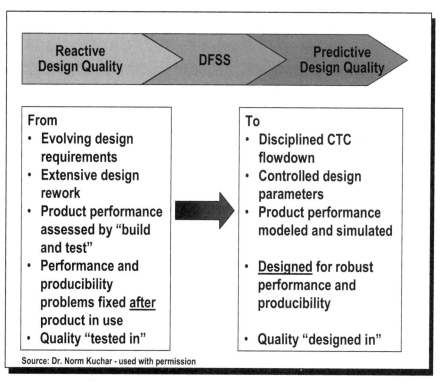

Figure 6.6 The Vision of DFSS

While Lean Six Sigma (DMAIC) fixes known problems, **DFSS prevents currently unknown problems from occurring downstream**. This is a strong statement, because sometimes we don't know what we don't know.

> *"As we know, there are known knowns. These are things we know we know. We also know there are known unknowns. That is to say we know there are some things we do not know. But there are also unknown unknowns, the ones we don't know we don't know."*
>
> Donald Rumsfeld
> Department of Defense news briefing
> February 12, 2002

Keep in mind that DFSS is not "up front" DMAIC. Although there is overlap in the thinking skills needed between DMAIC and DFSS and also in the tools, the working context is different. Teams work more in the world of the unknown during design and development than they do when problem solving in a production environment. We complete this section on the motivation for DFSS with one last comparison between Lean, Six Sigma, and DFSS. Recalling Table 5.3, Relationship Between Lean and Six Sigma (aka the Northeast Chart), we extend that chart to also include where DFSS fits into the picture. It is shown in Table 6.1. While our goal is to move in a northeasterly direction, DFSS allows us to move faster and more directly, simultaneously simplifying, perfecting, and innovating, to get to the higher yields.

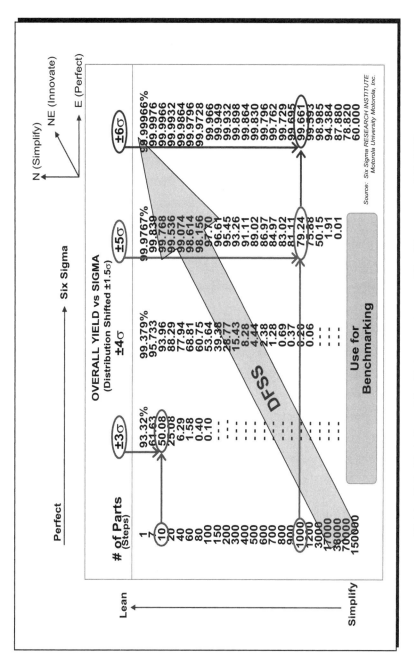

Table 6.1 Relationship Between Lean, Six Sigma, and DFSS

The DFSS (IDOV) Methodology

Like Lean Six Sigma (LSS), Design for Six Sigma (DFSS) employs a structured methodology that allows projects to be accomplished in a phased approach. Unlike LSS, however, the naming convention for the DFSS methodology is not as ingrained into the marketplace as DMAIC is for LSS. While one might see the acronyms DMADV, DCOV, ICOV, etc., associated with the DFSS methodology, we have elected to stay with the original terminology called IDOV. IDOV, which means Identify, Design, Optimize, and Validate, is the original term coined by Dr. Norm Kuchar at General Electric Corporate R&D when he and his team rolled out DFSS worldwide. Keep in mind these are only single words that describe what happens in a given phase of the DFSS methodology. What is important is what these words connote and what actually takes place in each of the phases. Figure 6.7 shows the major activities that should take place within each phase. These are the rectangles with the activity names inserted. These activities also form the major modules or chapters in our DFSS Capstone course. The bullet entries represent the deliverables that should be an output from each of the four major phases.

While it is beyond the scope of this text to delve deeply into each of the activities of the four phases, we will give a brief description of and provide the **Questions Leaders Must Ask** in each phase of IDOV. DFSS is a knowledge generating strategy designed to produce as much knowledge as possible early in the life cycle of a product or service. The questions provide the pull system for the application of the tools and techniques which, if used properly, will generate the answers to the questions and thus provide the required knowledge. The reader who has already seen the questions in Chapters 3 and 4 will note that these questions are very similar to those. However, many have been restated and extended to emphasize the need for this knowledge earlier in the lifecycle of a product or service.

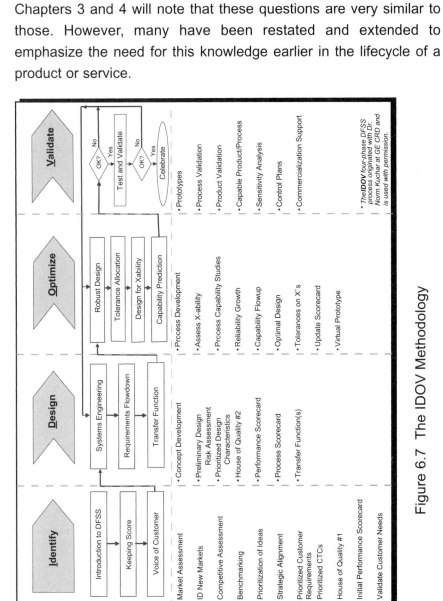

Figure 6.7 The IDOV Methodology

In the **Identify** phase, we identify potential markets for new or redesigned products and services and do a competitive/market assessment, benchmarking our results with market leaders. Our ideas are then prioritized, leading to our defining specific DFSS projects or studies that can be aligned with our market strategy. Customer requirements are then prioritized and Critical to Customer functional requirements (CTCs) identified. Customer needs should be validated with data and not be just somebody's opinion. Using a technique such as Quality Function Deployment (see House of Quality #1 in Figure 6.8), the functional performance CTCs can be prioritized.

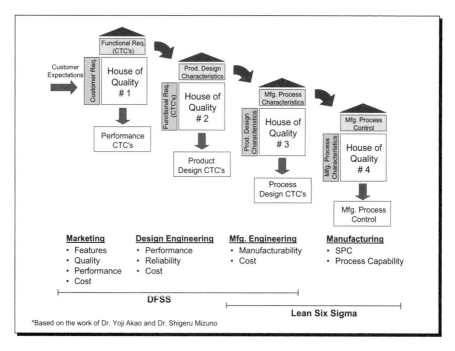

Figure 6.8 Quality Function Deployment*

These prioritized functional requirements then become an important input to House of Quality #2. As one can see, the marketing team plays a critical role in this phase, so if you may have thought that DFSS was just an engineering function, the activities in this phase should dispel any such notion. It is also important that the DFSS performance scorecard be initialized during this phase.

> *"If we're not keeping score, we're only practicing."*
>
> *Vince Lombardi*

The truth is we are not practicing. We are in a highly competitive global market where only the fittest survive. The knowledge needed to help us survive the Identify phase in any DFSS project is closely associated with the questions shown in Table 6.2. Please reference this table for a list of **Questions Leaders Must Ask in the Identify Phase**. Conversely, the answers to these questions must provide sufficient knowledge to be able to move to the next phase. These questions provide leadership a means of actively participating in the IDOV process so that they can help guide the overall execution of the project.

1. *Why are we working on this project? What need does the project address and how has the value been validated?*
(Continued on Next Page)

Table 6.2 Question Leaders Must Ask in the Identify Phase

2. *Who are the external customers who will benefit from this project and who are the customers who may not benefit? Furthermore, who are the internal stakeholders who could affect or be affected by this project? Have we done a stakeholder analysis? What does it say?*

3. *What are the prioritized functional requirements (CTCs or critical outputs) in measurable terms and how do they relate to the Voice of the Customer data?*

4. *How will we determine success of the project? What are the measurable attributes of this project and what are the goals associated with those measures?*

5. *Do measurement systems currently exist to support this project? If so, what is the measurement system capability?*

6. *Have the performance CTCs been entered into the DFSS Scorecard with any existing data? If there is data, does it have integrity?*

7. *What kind of gap exists between the current performance and the requirements/goals? What is the risk associated with this gap?*

8. *Do we have the appropriate people to undertake this project and do they have the appropriate skills? What are the resource gaps in terms of people, skills, machines, IT support, etc.? And what are the competing activities for these resources?*

Table 6.2 Question Leaders Must Ask in the Identify Phase

In the **Design** phase, we flow the prioritized critical functional requirements down to specific design parameters. Again, Quality Function Deployment can be used to accomplish this. House of Quality #2 in Figure 6.8 helps us do that. We formulate design concepts by creating alternative designs that fulfill the functional CTCs. Conceptual design tools such as TRIZ (an acronym for Russian words that, when translated, mean Theory of Inventive Problem Solving), Axiomatic Design, and Pugh Concept Selection can be used to facilitate the process. Preliminary design risk assessments are also accomplished using tools like a design FMEA (Failure Mode and Effect Analysis). The technical, cost, schedule, market, and political risks must be evaluated. A set of prioritized design characteristics is a key output of this phase. These design parameters are then linked to the functional performance CTCs via what is called a **transfer function**. Figure 6.9 illustrates the concept of a transfer function. It is a mathematical representation of the relationship between a y (CTC) and the design parameters, or x's, that influence y. A simple example of a transfer function for total processing time (y) in a loan generation activity that involves three departments might be $y = x_1 + x_2 + x_3$, where x_i represents the processing time for department i and i = 1, 2, 3. Not all transfer functions are as simple as this one nor as easily obtained. Transfer functions are also referred to as prediction models or mathematical models.

The transfer function is the critical link that helps us establish relationships between the performance CTCs and the design parameters. One cannot overestimate the value of a good transfer function, because if we have them, a whole new world of optimization becomes real very quickly. One of the biggest technical challenges in DFSS is the generation of good transfer functions, and one of the biggest cultural challenges in DFSS is to convince leadership of the need for developing transfer functions. In fact, the maturity of a DFSS initiative is correlated to the percentage of performance CTCs for which we have validated transfer functions. Transfer functions should also be developed for a CTC's standard deviation (σ).

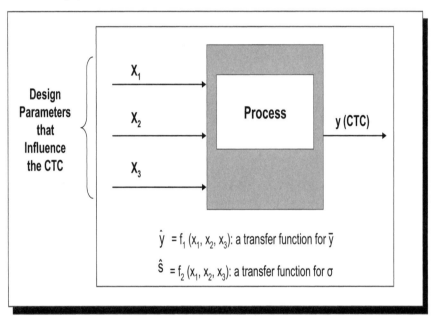

Figure 6.9 Transfer Functions

If transfer functions are so vitally important, then where do we get them? Exact transfer functions can sometimes be obtained from the literature or from theory. For example, an electrical engineer knows that the impedance (Z) through a 2-resistor circuit is given by $Z = (R_1 \cdot R_2) / (R_1 + R_2)$, where R_1 and R_2 represent the resistance in ohms of the two resistors, respectively. Developing theoretical models can be time-consuming and assumption-laden and thus can be problematic. More often than not, the most useful transfer functions are approximations of the true, but unknown, transfer function and these approximating transfer functions can be obtained by using Design of Experiments (DOE). DOE is the most preferable means of finding transfer functions, because it is efficient and very effective. An organization will never be proficient in DFSS if its practitioners do not know DOE. If transfer functions represent the fire of innovation in DFSS, then DOE is the ignitor. DOE is sometimes used in conjunction with simulation and historical data to generate transfer functions. However obtained, validated transfer functions are key.

Table 6.3 provides the list of **Questions Leaders Must Ask in the Design phase.**

---

1. *What are the conceptual designs and associated technologies necessary to support the functional requirements?*

2. *What are the risks associated with these designs with regard to cost, schedule, quality, etc.? Have we accomplished an FMEA (Failure Mode and Effect Analysis) on the prospective designs and/or performed a Pugh Concept Selection?*

3. *What are the potential tradeoffs to eliminate the projected failure modes?*

4. *Have we completed a requirements flowdown, while maintaining clear links to the performance CTCs?*

(Continued on Next Page)

Table 6.3 Questions Leaders Must Ask in the Design Phase

5. *What are the key input variables (or parameters) that affect the mean and the standard deviation of the measures of performance (the CTCs)? And what kind of flexibility do we have for manipulating them?*

6. *What are the transfer functions for each of the critical outputs or CTCs? And what is the current and projected capability of these performance measures?*

7. *Have the DFSS Performance and Process Scorecards been updated with the latest information based on the knowledge gained from this phase?*

Table 6.3 Questions Leaders Must Ask in the Design Phase

Before moving on to the Optimize phase, leaders must demand that these questions have been adequately addressed and answered.

In the **Optimize** phase, we capitalize on the knowledge that has already been generated in the previous phases. In particular, we can use transfer functions to optimize the performance of the functional performance CTCs. Three major activities in this phase that utilize the transfer function are *Expected Value Analysis, Parameter (or Robust) Design, and Tolerance Allocation.* In LSS, we consider the variability in the critical outputs or CTCs in great detail. In DFSS, particularly in this phase, we also consider variability in the inputs or design parameters as well. This is a major shift from the classic LSS thought process. The next three paragraphs provide a moderately technical description of these three tools which make use of a transfer function and show how DFSS is considerably different from LSS.

Expected Value Analysis (EVA) is the analytical process of determining the output (or y) distribution–including its shape, mean, and standard deviation–under conditions where the input parameters vary according to specific distributions. This is often not an intuitive process, and we illustrate this fact with an example to show why EVA is needed. Let's suppose we have a very simple transfer function, one that most readers have encountered in the past, namely $y = x^2$. That is, when x = 5, then y = 25; when x = 6, then y = 36, etc. Let's further assume that x varies according to a normal distribution with a mean of 6 and a standard deviation of 2, as shown in Figure 6.10. What will the mean (or expected value) of the output (y) be and what will the distribution of y look like? One might conclude that y's distribution will be normally distributed with a mean of 36 (because the mean of x is 6 and we are squaring it). However, the true result is that the distribution of y is not normal and neither is the mean equal to 36.

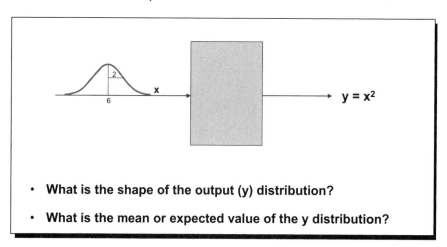

- **What is the shape of the output (y) distribution?**
- **What is the mean or expected value of the y distribution?**

Figure 6.10 Expected Value Analysis Example

The point here is that strange things can happen when the distributional aspects of the input parameters are taken into consideration. That is, we may not get the result we are expecting. While analytical techniques can be used to generate the results of an EVA, we highly recommend the use of software like DFSS Master (an Excel add-in) to perform EVA and generate the results much more quickly. Please see the information on recommended software in the Reference section of this text for easy application of LSS and DFSS tools and techniques.

Parameter (or Robust) Design finds the **optimal location parameter (i.e., the mean)** of the input parameter distributions in order to maximize the performance capability of the CTC performance measures. *Tolerance Allocation* finds **which of the input parameters' standard deviations** should be tightened and which can be relaxed to maximize performance capability. These techniques allow the designer to perform cost/benefit tradeoffs through the assignment of specific **means and standard deviations** to the design parameters. As with EVA, the use of software is highly recommended to accomplish both of these activities. Many leaders think that their organizations already do "robust design," etc., and that may indeed be the case. Our experience indicates that if an organization has that capability, it is pretty much localized to a small group of experts who are enlisted to help if and when the need should arise. Our belief is that anyone working in a design capacity should know and be able to use these concepts quickly as part of their daily regimen. This means knowing the best tools available to make the implementation of these methods quick and easy.

Once parameter design and tolerance allocation have taken place, we must assess the manufacturing capability. Even though the design may appear to be optimized, if we cannot build it or produce it, we will still have problems. The design community is responsible for communicating to manufacturing those critical variables or factors that must be tightly controlled and those parameters that may not have to be so tightly monitored. Conversely, manufacturing must know their production capability. Thus, process capability studies may have to be conducted and that information communicated to the designers. It should be apparent by now that DFSS is much more than just a design function. Marketing and manufacturing play significant roles in the DFSS process as well. We conclude the discussion on the optimize phase by providing a set of **Questions Leaders Must Ask in the Optimize Phase**. These are shown in Table 6.4.

---

1. *Have we performed parameter (robust) design and done tolerance allocation? What are the optimal values for all of the design parameters?*

2. *How sensitive is the CTC performance measure to changes in the parameters? Have we accomplished a sensitivity analysis and passed those results on to manufacturing?*

3. *What are the sources of variability in the system? Which are controllable and which are not? How do we control them and what is our method of documenting and maintaining this control?*

4. *Are any of the sources of variability supplier dependent? If so, what is the plan to minimize supplier variability and its impact on the system? What are the costs involved in doing so?*

(Continued on Next Page)

Table 6.4 Question Leaders Must Ask in the Optimize Phase

> 5. *Have we confirmed via process capability studies that the design is indeed producible?*
>
> 6. *What gaps and risks still exist in the design? What is the action plan to close those gaps and reduce the risks?*
>
> 7. *Have we updated the DFSS Scorecard with the knowledge obtained from this phase?*

Table 6.4 Question Leaders Must Ask in the Optimize Phase

In the **Validate** phase, we must verify that both product and process function as specified. We must be able to confirm that product and process capability are as predicted in the DFSS Scorecard, which reflects all of the knowledge generated from the project thus far. Prototypes may be needed to assist us in comparing the actual capability with the predicted capability. If the capability is not confirmed, then gap analysis must be accomplished. The gap analysis will suggest what our next steps should be. Reasons gaps exist include inadequate transfer functions, input design parameter variability not properly characterized, Voice of the Customer (VOC) requirements gathering and flowdown not properly conducted, and extraneous variation inadequately controlled due to poor Standard Operating Procedures (SOPs) or SOPs not being followed. If and when the capability is confirmed, all drawings, sensitivity analyses, and associated knowledge must be passed to manufacturing. Process flow and control systems are also developed in this phase and deployed to manufacturing. The **Questions Leaders Must Ask in the Validate Phase** are given in Table 6.5. Satisfactory answers to these questions will ensure that the resulting design of the product or service has passed through the combined scrutiny of marketing, conceptual design, detailed design, and manufacturing.

1. *What validation testing has been completed and what are the results?*

2. *Is there a significant gap between the actual capability and the predicted capability from the DFSS Scorecard? If so, what are the next steps to bridge that gap?*

3. *What is the gap between current performance and the customer requirements (the CTCs)? What differences, if any, still remain?*

4. *Has the production system been put under a state of quality control? What are the capability measures, such as Cp, Cpk, and Defects per Unit (DPU)?*

5. *What are the potential problems and/or unintended consequences of the design? What are the preventative and contingency actions to address them?*

6. *How has all of this information been documented and communicated to the appropriate people (stakeholders, service, training, manufacturing, etc.)?*

7. *Have drawings, sensitivity analyses and associated knowledge been shared and passed on to manufacturing?*

8. *What is the total project benefit in terms of quantified quality, cost, and delivery measures?*

Table 6.5 Questions Leaders Must Ask in the Validate Phase

Like LSS, DFSS also has a set of tools and techniques that can and should be used to help answer the questions in each of the phases. Leadership cannot expect their people to answer these questions without empowering them with the ability to get the answers. Figure 6.11 shows the tools and techniques that are commonly used in each of the IDOV phases.

Identify	Design	Optimize	Validate
Project or Study Charter	Assign Specifications to CTC's	Histogram	Sensitivity Analysis
Strategic Plan	Axiomatic Design	Distributional Analysis	Gap Analysis
Cross-Functional Team	Customer Interviews	Empirical Data Distribution	FMEA
Voice of the Customer	Formulate Design Concepts	Expected Value Analysis (EVA)	Fault Tree Analysis
Customer Retention Grid	Pugh Concept Generation	Adding Noise to EVA	Control Plan
Benchmarking	TRIZ	Non-Normal Output Distributions	PF/CE/CNX/SOP
KANO's Model	FMEA	Design of Experiments	Run/Control Charts
Questionnaires	Fault Tree Analysis	Multiple Response Optimization	Mistake Proofing
Focus Groups	Brainstorming	Robust Design Development	MSA
Interviews	QFD	Using S-hat Model	Reaction Plan
Internet Search	Scorecard	Using Interaction Plots	High Throughput Testing
Historical Data Analysis	Transfer Function	Using Contour Plots	
Design of Experiments	Design of Experiments	Parameter Design	
Quality Function Deployment	Deterministic Simulators	Tolerance Allocation	
Pairwise Comparison	Discrete Event Simulation	Design For Manufacturability and Assembly	
Analytical Hierarchy Process	Confidence Intervals	Mistake Proofing	
Performance Scorecard	Hypothesis Testing	Product Capability Prediction	
Flow Charts	MSA	Part, Process, and SW Scorecard	
FMEA	Computer Aided Design	Risk Assessment	
Visualization	Computer Aided Engineering	Reliability	
		Multidisciplinary Design Optimization (MDO)	

Figure 6.11 Design for Six Sigma Tools and Techniques

If one compares this figure with Figure 5.7, Lean Six Sigma Tools and Techniques, you will see an overlap of the sets of tools and techniques used within DMAIC and IDOV. For example, Design of Experiments (DOE) is a tool that is heavily used in DFSS or IDOV, but it also is used in LSS or DMAIC. This overlap of tools between IDOV and DMAIC is not unexpected and is evidence of the evolutionary development of the two methodologies. However, some of the more automated tools such as *Expected Value Analysis, Parameter Design, and Tolerance Allocation* are uniquely applicable to DFSS, because they can be used early in the lifecycle of a product or service. Although this text does not address the tools in any depth, we highly encourage the reader to refer to the texts and software in the Reference section of this book for more detailed information on the use of the tools and techniques discussed here.

While IDOV is often used for designing new products and processes, it can also be used to redesign existing products and processes. Many times the traditional DMAIC strategy produces results that are less than optimum and/or do not satisfy the customer requirements. In these cases, IDOV provides a valuable alternative or "next step" beyond the DMAIC methodology. This phenomenon is depicted in Figure 6.12.

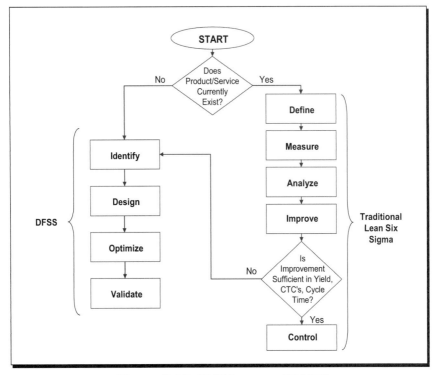

Figure 6.12 IDOV versus DMAIC

In general, the DMAIC approach and tools work best when the goal is to improve an existing product or process, with baseline performance measures already in place or at least available. The IDOV approach and tools work best when the goal is to design a new product or process, with no baseline performance measures available, or when redesigning an existing product or process that is not meeting the performance requirements. Many projects contain elements of both, so we recommend the use of the appropriate tools no matter what banner they may be placed under. If the goal is to generate knowledge from the pull of the knowledge generating questions that have been provided here (which the goal should be), then there will be less debate over whether it is called DMAIC or IDOV.

Best Practices in Deploying DFSS

As a result of helping many organizations deploy and implement DFSS, even before it may have been called that, we have accumulated a set of best practices over the years. While every deployment is different, these best practices apply to all of them, regardless of the culture and uniqueness of the organization. Here are our top ten best practices that will apply to any organization:

1. *Educate the leadership in DFSS to build organizational commitment and momentum. Without leadership's active involvement and participation, it will be difficult to gain and maintain momentum. If we expect leaders to be actively engaged in it, they need to know what "it" is.*

2. *Begin using the DFSS tools and techniques on all product developments and redesigns, no matter where in the life cycle a product may be. Do not wait until you have the perfect team assembled. Train your DFSS Belts and get them using the tools immediately.*

3. *Weave the DFSS tools and techniques into your own design and development process. It is better to integrate IDOV into your existing new product development process than it is to scrap your current system and replace it with IDOV. This text does not advocate the latter.*

4. *Continuously review progress based on DFSS projects and deployment metrics and realign if necessary. Project reviews which utilize the questions in each phase are key to project success and, ultimately, business success.*

5. *Build the bridge to innovation: the transfer function. We have said it before and will repeat it again: transfer functions can be the biggest technical challenge in rolling out DFSS, but without them, the rollout is doomed. Transfer functions are the key to detailed design and optimization, and they are a phenomenally compact way of storing huge amounts of critical knowledge. Build a culture of developing transfer functions and you will build a DFSS culture.*

6. *Design of Experiments (DOE) knowledge is critical, so build a strong capability in the right DOE methods. By "right methods" of DOE, we mean a blending of all of the best of the best DOE techniques available today. Traditional factorial types of designs, as well as Taguchi designs, must be included, and the practitioner needs to know which technique to use when. Remember, DOE is the driver for transfer function development.*

7. *Establish a good process capability and parts database: "in-house" and suppliers. This will help establish the DFSS Scorecard for many products and services.*

8. *Directly link DFSS to **business success**, e.g., financial benefits. Leadership is the key to making this happen and **must** make it happen.*

9. *Partner with someone who truly knows what DFSS is and has a proven record of motivating people throughout the education and coaching process, all while producing results. Do not underestimate the motivational aspect involved in the education and coaching sessions. Even professionals need to be motivated.*

10. *View DFSS as a cultural change – a mindset, not just a tool set.*

Financial Accountability

DFSS should impact both the top-line (revenue) and the bottom-line (profitability) financial metrics of an organization. However, it must be recognized that hard dollar savings will be more difficult to measure in DFSS than in LSS. Since much of the DFSS work is done in the design and development phases of the life cycle of a product or service, it makes sense that it may take years to accurately validate the savings and ROI on a particular product or service. However, good financial estimates can still be obtained. We provide the reader with several ways to estimate the financial savings from a DFSS IDOV project.

First, we can compare the unoptimized DFSS Scorecard at the beginning of a DFSS project with the optimized scorecard at the end of the project. We can calculate the difference in yield, number produced each year, cost per defect, etc., from the scorecard because all of the data needed to do so is or should be contained in the scorecard. Since the DFSS Scorecard provides a running history of how improvements are being made with regard to performance, parts, processes, and software, capability changes in each of these four areas can be tracked over the duration of the project.

We can also compare the current project's area under the resource curve with previously launched products' areas under the resource curve. Recall or revisit Figure 6.5 (The Benefits of DFSS) and note that for any product, such a curve can be constructed and thus be compared with similarly launched products in the past. In such comparisons, total resources can be estimated and should include human resources, capital assets, redesign efforts, etc. Not every resource can be accurately accounted for, but by using sampling and other LSS concepts, like expected value and confidence intervals, we can get good estimates of the total resource costs.

There is always a cost per day of failing to launch a product on target. For every day that we beat the target, consider that as top-line growth. If everyone on the design team was aware of this cost from the start, it will have an impact on the team's performance. Cost of Poor Quality (COPQ) saved on redesigns is easily computed, and Cost of Lost Opportunity can also be computed for such things as a regulatory agency pulling a product from the market or we lose a customer to a competitor due to issues with quality, cost, or delivery. Increased market share can be tracked over time; and just being able to enter a market because we used DFSS, whereas without it we couldn't, also has financial implications. DFSS should also lead to a reduced number of prototypes due to the emphasis on modeling and simulation versus the build and test mentality. That is, good transfer functions will reduce the number of prototypes and associated testing and maintenance that goes along with building prototypes.

Implementation Accountability

While financial accountability is desired in DFSS, it is well known that accounting for savings in DFSS is typically a longer-term process than it is in LSS. A shorter-term accountability that is almost immediately measurable is implementation accountability. That is, are we successfully implementing the methodology and tools of DFSS? Project completion cycle time is extremely important, and in LSS, DMAIC projects should take absolutely no longer than 6 months. However, if we are going to do a complete IDOV cycle on a product or service, it is conceivable that such an activity could last longer than a year and maybe even two. Remember that marketing, engineering, and manufacturing are all necessarily involved in the IDOV process. Considering that most companies cannot and will not wait a year or more to see the results from an application of IDOV, we have introduced the concept of a "study" into the DFSS lexicon. A study is the execution and completion of work which utilizes one of the DFSS tools or methods as part of an assignment to meet overall unit objectives. A study can be accomplished in a much shorter period of time. Whereas a DFSS **project** implies the completion of all four phases of the IDOV methodology on some unit, a DFSS **study** represents a smaller entity of work that could contribute to an overall project or could stand on its own. The purpose of studies is to help gain quick hitting successes and to build maturity in the DFSS tools and methodology. The differences between a project and a study are summarized in Figure 6.13.

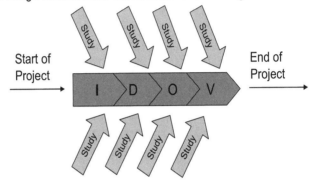

Project
- This is an effort that results in the design of a part, sub-assembly, module or system. The design process passes through all four phases of IDOV, starting with the concept and customer requirements and ending with a validated design that has been delivered to manufacturing.

Study
- This is the execution and completion of work which applies one of the DFSS tools / methods as part of an assignment to meet design objectives. A study does not proceed through all 4 phases of IDOV.

Source: George Maszle (Xerox Corporation) - used with permission

Figure 6.13 Project versus Study

Like both LSS and DFSS projects, a DFSS study requires a charter or contract at the outset plus leadership commitment and support to complete. DFSS studies must contribute to the business objectives and contribute to the knowledge acquisition of the DFSS process by answering at least one or two of the **Questions Leaders Must Ask**. Table 6.6 shows some of the areas in which many of our clients have accomplished DFSS studies. Specific tool application in each of these areas is a common type of DFSS study, because the proper application of the tool will deliver the required piece of knowledge.

- Establishing and Populating a DFSS Scorecard (Identify)

- Understanding the True Voice of the Customer (Identify)

- Concept Generation (Design)

- Translating the Voice of the Customer: Requirements Flowdown (Design)

- Transfer Functions (Design)

- Robust and Optimized Designs that can be produced efficiently and with high quality (Optimize)

- Rolling up the Results/Validating the Design (Validate)

Table 6.6 Implementation Areas for DFSS Studies

We have found the DFSS study concept to be extremely valuable. It has helped jump start many DFSS initiatives by gaining critical mass and crucial momentum in leadership support and commitment for DFSS. The impatience of today's economy demands quick hitting successes which these studies provide. Over time, as the double-humped curve in Figure 6.5 becomes the single-humped curve shifted to the left, more and more of the DFSS efforts will move into the project arena. The projects will also be applied to larger and larger units, like modules and systems vis-à-vis parts and sub-assemblies. Figure 6.14 shows what maturation in DFSS looks like. This figure can also serve as a template for measuring the maturity of DFSS in an organization. If we are maturing in DFSS, we should see more of the studies and projects taking place in the northeast (upper right) part of this chart. It is leadership's responsibility to drive the DFSS initiative in a northeasterly direction. Maintaining our focus on generating the right kinds of knowledge (via the **Questions Leaders Must Ask**) is the key to DFSS maturity.

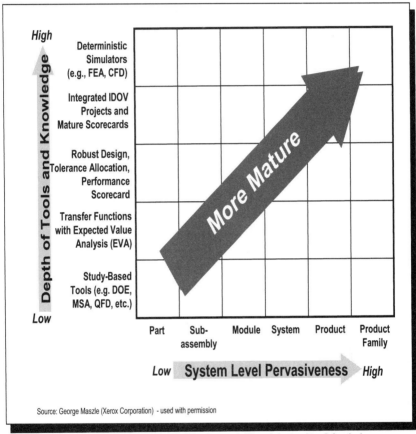

Source: George Maszle (Xerox Corporation) - used with permission

Figure 6.14 A DFSS Capability Maturity Model

What does a successful DFSS rollout look like? We conclude this section and chapter with an annotated list of recommendations for achieving a successful DFSS rollout.

Key Attributes of a Successful DFSS Rollout

1. Use projects and studies to link certification with competency. Your DFSS Belts will want to be certified, and certification must require project or study work. Approve projects and studies that drive your business to the desired state. Do not approve projects or studies for academic demonstration purposes. To further the certification/competency link, require that DFSS Belts demonstrate competency in all of the major activity areas (rectangles) of the IDOV methodology shown in Figure 6.7. Belt candidates must also be competent in the use of DFSS software and in coaching and mentoring. Competency must be demonstrated via projects or studies, but for some of the areas, prior work experience coupled with teachbacks to their DFSS coach may be accepted. Certification in DFSS must be competency based, and that competency must be demonstrated via projects and studies in many areas. The coach or mentor of a DFSS Belt candidate must sign off on every area, thereby affirming that the Belt candidate is competent in that particular area.

2. The DFSS tools and methods need to become part of the practitioner's "everyday" regimen. DFSS is much different in this regard than LSS. DFSS requires a greater depth of knowledge in its tools and methods than LSS does. The DFSS tools and methods must be so ingrained in the

practitioner that there will be no hesitancy to use them. When the required knowledge is needed, a DFSS Belt will know precisely which tool to use and will use it automatically, without necessarily imbedding its use in a project or study. That is the type of culture we are trying to develop, and that is why competency in the depth of the tools is needed, not only in using the tool itself but also in immediate recognition of when that tool should be used.

3. Use a highly motivational and easy-to-digest education program for bringing DFSS into your organization. That includes easy-to-use software like SPC XL, DOE Pro, and DFSS Master. If we can motivate our practitioners to use these tools to generate knowledge and success at the very beginning of their DFSS lives, the successes so generated will provide a motivation that will sustain itself throughout that person's lifetime.

4. Coaching is the key to competency, and this is the area that many organizations are unwilling to commit resources to. DFSS coaches must be master teachers and practitioners of DFSS, having done many projects and demonstrated success in all of the areas of DFSS. They must be motivators and have a passion for what they do. The need for sustained coaching in DFSS is an order of magnitude higher than it is in LSS, and it requires a corresponding level of expertise from its coaches. The number one failure mode for a stalled DFSS initiative is an organization's lack of commitment and dedication to a sustained coaching regimen for its Belt candidates.

To summarize this chapter, DFSS will challenge us to think differently; work differently; ask questions and challenge the status quo; make decisions with facts and data; and will demand the use of new principles, tools, and methodologies. When compared to reactive (pre-DFSS) design strategies, the more predictive IDOV methodology demonstrates its value by significantly reducing total life cycle resources, reducing time to market, and increasing revenue growth rate after product launch. In short, DFSS is a knowledge generating strategy geared toward extraordinary return on investment: a way to delight the customer and gain market share. If Lean Six Sigma has become the way we work, DFSS is the way we win.

Chapter 7

A COMPETITIVE EXCELLENCE MODEL

"Knowledge is Power."

Francis Bacon

We have just examined the underlying philosophies and methodologies of the Lean Six Sigma (LSS) and Design for Six Sigma (DFSS) improvement strategies. One very important attribute that has made both of these knowledge generating strategies successful is the infrastructure in which they are deployed. In this chapter we address the overall system in which the infrastructures of LSS and DFSS are imbedded. In other words, we take the concept of knowledge generation to the enterprise level, a level of abstraction higher than what we have been addressing thus far. Operating at the enterprise level, we are much better able to see the vision of where LSS and DFSS should be taking us and where in the big picture of business these improvement strategies exist. Sometimes we are so engrossed in the minutiae of a LSS project that we fail to understand why we are really doing this and to what aspect of the business plan we are really contributing. Every corporate business leader we know is concerned not only about the current state of his or her business, but also the future state. LSS and DFSS are concerned with the current and future states of products, services, processes, and value streams, but how do we look at the current and future states of a business enterprise? That is the subject of this chapter. Please reference Figure 7.1.

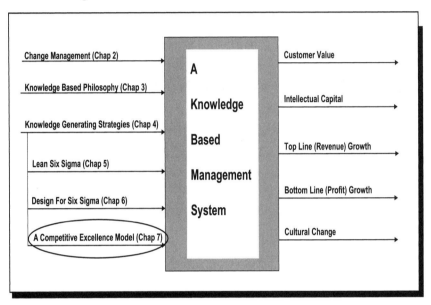

Figure 7.1 KBM IPO Diagram

To address this topic, we introduce the concept of a competitive excellence model. The model described in this chapter originates from the performance excellence work of Dr. Michael Slocum. It takes into consideration all of the ingredients that are needed to make a business system function properly. This model will provide the reader with a knowledge generating strategy at the enterprise level that builds upon the knowledge generating strategies we have already touched on. It can serve as a vision, as well as a game plan, for any organization wanting to establish an enterprise-level improvement strategy.

The Air Academy Associates Competitive Excellence Model (A³CE Model) is a strategic business model designed to guide organizations to a state of "competitive excellence." Competitive excellence means the ability to survive the current demands of the marketplace and to evolve the business to a state of continued and expanded success. Competitive excellence necessarily comprises strategic excellence, operational excellence, process excellence, design excellence, and innovation excellence. The A^3CE Model provides our clients with the plan, strategy, and tactics – including the methods, tools, and techniques – needed to survive and evolve. This means maintaining or improving current levels of business performance while evolving to an innovative business culture capable of achieving the next level of performance: decreased development times; highly capable and exciting products and services; structured creativity; and growth. The A^3CE Model is presented graphically in Figure 7.2. Please refer to this graphic as we describe its major components.

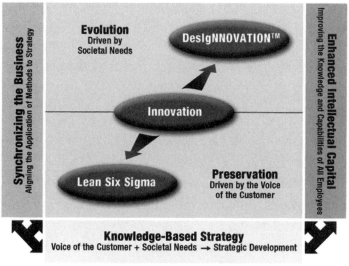

© 2006 Air Academy Associates

Figure 7.2 The A^3CE Model

The foundation of the A³CE Model is our Knowledge Based Business Strategy, an approach that uses knowledge to orchestrate the strategic direction the business will take as it focuses on both customer and societal needs. The model incorporates organizational and employee enhancement, as well as process, product, and business innovation. The key piece of knowledge in this strategy is to know at any moment in time which activities and what resources need to be allocated to the two major domains of any business. The A³CE Model refers to these two domains as Preservation and Evolution. Every activity that a business conducts should contribute to either the Preservation or Evolution domains (or goals) of an organization.

"Preservation" describes those activities that maintain or protect the current market position of a business. It means maintaining the market share, profitability, and brand recognition. It also means extending the net profitability period of a given product or service to achieve its maximum maturity capability through continuous and incremental improvement efforts. Preservation is driven by the voice of the customer and demands a clear understanding of that voice.

"Evolution" is the set of activities focused on the development of new products or services. This means taking the company to new areas of endeavor and developing discontinuous technologies. Evolution is the ability of a business to recreate itself by developing new life cycle curves for new products/services or new generations of products/services. Evolution requires breakthrough improvements for the purpose of starting a new life cycle curve for a product or service. Evolution is driven by societal needs which are not in the customer's current vocabulary.

Please reference Figure 7.3 to see how Preservation and Evolution relate to the natural Biological S-Curve for products and services. After a product or service is conceived, it progresses through a cycle of knowledge building, eventually passing through adolescence on its way to maturity. Preservation activities attempt to extend maturity as long as possible, but as the decline phase is anticipated and entered, we continue to use preservation techniques to extend the life cycle further by adding features and capitalizing on our knowledge of the voice of the customer to create new inflection points on the curve. Due to many factors, including technological change, the number of new "humps" that can be temporarily induced is extremely limited. Evolution provides for the starting of a new life cycle, but it is one which does not begin at "ground zero."

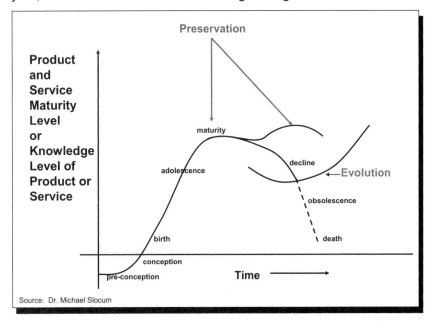

Figure 7.3 How Preservation and Evolution Relate to the Biological S-Curve

The knowledge gained from previous life cycles should allow a new evolutionary curve to begin at a point much higher in the knowledge/maturity scale than previous life cycles. This is also depicted in Figure 7.3.

The knowledge based strategy needs to support both the Preservation and Evolution states, because both are needed if a company wants to survive and prosper. Without adequate knowledge of the Voice of the Customer and Societal Needs, strategic development will be flawed and could potentially take an enterprise down the wrong path. The knowledge based strategy must dictate the required bias between the two domains. For example, at the outset of a competitive excellence initiative, one company may be more biased toward the Preservation state and use LSS heavily as its knowledge generating strategy. Another company may be striving for a more balanced state by concurrently using LSS, DFSS, and Innovation techniques. Currently, the trend seems to be that the Preservation state is more heavily weighted for many companies, perhaps because of increased global competition and inherently poor internal processes that sap a company's resources.

Most improvement strategies today emphasize the need for understanding the Voice of the Customer. Unfortunately, that voice is sometimes not easy to understand or interpret. While customers can adequately state preferences and tell us what they like and dislike about a product or service, it is extremely difficult for customers to anticipate or predict what the societal needs are going to be over the next decade, and we cannot expect them to do so. Surveys, interviews, and focus groups are not able to extract this kind of information.

Understanding and anticipating societal needs must play a critical role in the Evolution domain of any enterprise. Providers of products and services must continually assess the variables that are affecting and will affect society and link them to new technologies and capabilities. If Union Pacific had been in the "transportation" business rather than the "railroad" business, we might be flying Union Pacific today instead of United, American, or some other airline. Continuing on the theme of transportation, exactly when was the wheel invented? Some 5,000 years ago. How long has the suitcase (or luggage) been around? Also thousands of years. How long have suitcases or luggage with wheels on them been around? Not since societal needs dictated that these two concepts be combined in the size, shape, and fashion required by more modern means of traveling.

A controlled process of systematic innovation is needed to repeatably, predictably, and reliably create new products and services that link technology to societal needs, and furthermore, develop technology that will satisfy societal needs. Extending beyond the voice of the customer, societal needs represent the "heart and soul" of customers and are the key drivers in the Evolution domain.

> *"A consumer can seldom say today what new product or new service would be desirable and useful to him three years from now, or a decade from now... new product and new service has been accomplished in every case in my experience by application of innovation and knowledge."*
>
> *W. Edwards Deming*
> **Out of the Crisis**

While the Knowledge Based Strategy forms the foundation of the A3CE Model, there are two major pillars attached to the base plate that bound the two operational domains of Preservation and Evolution. Synchronizing the Business, the pillar on the left in Figure 7.4, aligns the methods and intended practitioners of those methods with the strategy. If the strategy leans heavily toward the Preservation state, then the knowledge generating approach will fall more into the Lean Six Sigma improvement strategy and methodology. If the strategy is more biased toward the Evolution domain, more emphasis will be put on the DesIgNNOVATION™ methodology.

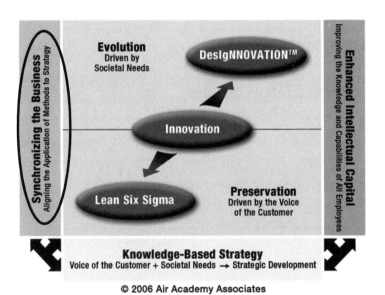

© 2006 Air Academy Associates

Figure 7.4 The A3CE Model

DesIgNNOVATION™ is a term that embodies the Design for Six Sigma and Axiomatic Design methodologies as well as the related Innovation techniques such as TRIZ and others that will be needed to reliably predict and satisfy societal needs. Note that the Innovation methodology is integrally linked to both Preservation and Evolution by way of the Lean Six Sigma and DesIgNNOVATION™ tracks. That is, innovation, be it strategic or tactical, will play an important role in both domains.

To effectively align the applications of the methods with the strategy requires training and coaching in synchronizing the business. There are effective and easy-to-use tools that can assist us in this alignment process. Participants who play pivotal roles in the synchronizing process include the executives, finance, human resources, information technology, project management, and communications. Tasks addressed in the synchronizing process include deployment planning to capture the vision and goals and to understand the boundaries for what will be supported and what will not be supported in the deployment. Synchronizing the business also means leadership alignment and getting all of the business operations engaged in the rollout of whatever performance improvement strategies may be employed.

The second pillar of the A³CE Model, Enhanced Intellectual Capital, is shown on the right in Figure 7.5. Building intellectual capital is what competitive excellence is all about, so essentially, this is the output or response variable at the enterprise level of all the activities that contribute to competitive excellence. This part of the model concerns itself with improving the knowledge and capabilities of **all** employees. Unlike many LSS or DFSS strategies that target only certain people (like Belts) for training, the A³CE Model requires that all employees be involved in bringing an enterprise up to a higher level of intellectual capital. If any organization wants to deem itself "competitively excellent," it cannot do so without the participation of everyone. Maybe not at first, but ultimately everyone will be involved and will receive some level of education or training designed to improve their knowledge levels of their processes

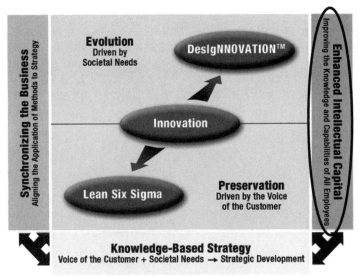

Figure 7.5 The A³CE Model

and products. The Intellectual Capital pillar of the A³CE Model interacts with the Knowledge Based Strategy base plate and the Synchronizing the Business pillar, shown by the triple-arrow connectors at the bottom corners of Figure 7.6, to form a framework and alignment mechanism for the execution of the strategy.

No model can be complete without considering the execution of its strategy. The execution of the competitive excellence strategy is symbolized in Figure 7.6 by the three major methodological tracks (shown as large ovals in the graphic). These three sets of methods correspond to the capabilities that are transferred to the practitioners by way of education, training, application, and coaching. The three tracks provide the synergy required to support both the Preservation and Evolution states of the business.

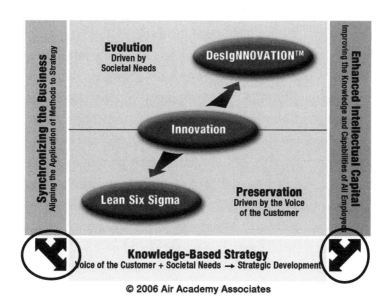

Figure 7.6 The A³CE Model

Lean Six Sigma and the DMAIC methodology represent the best knowledge generating improvement strategy available today to support the Preservation domain. We have numerous offerings and certifications within this track, as described in Chapter 5. The DesIgNNOVATION™ track supports the Evolution domain and consists of DFSS and the IDOV methodology, which was described in detail in Chapter 6, along with innovation methodologies like TRIZ. While a detailed discussion of TRIZ is beyond the scope of this text, a brief description is provided to give the reader a glimpse of this powerful method.

TRIZ, pronounced like "trees," is an acronym for the Russian equivalent of Theory of Inventive Problem Solving. TRIZ is a result of the work of Genrich Altshuller, a Russian patent inspector, who in 1946 began a massive statistical affinitization process by analyzing hundreds of thousands of patents. His work turned immense amounts of data into the following knowledge: he found that almost all of the world's patents recorded solutions that could be characterized as solving contradictions involving the same recurring 39 problem parameters. He further found that the solutions to these contradictions involved 40 recurring inventive principles. So imagine, if you can, a problem that has the following contradiction: we want to increase the "strength" of a material but that causes the problem of "more weight." Strength and weight are two of TRIZ's 39 problem parameters. A classic example of this is the strength and weight of the body armor that a soldier carries. We want more strength (i.e., protection), but we don't want the additional weight (in fact, we would like the weight to be even less than the current weight). This is a contradiction involving these two problem parameters. Altshuller's analysis found that 4 of the 40 inventive principles were used to solve this particular contradiction. Thus, we have now narrowed our search for a problem solution down to potentially 4 inventive principles that have been used to solve this problem before. What TRIZ does for us in the innovation domain is to help us **converge** on a solution rather than broaden our scope of potential solutions via **divergent** techniques which tend to dominate the current way of creative thinking. TRIZ can be done on a strategic level as well as at the tactical level. Thus, it can be used to generate conceptual designs in the Design phase of IDOV in DFSS, for example, as well as find a solution to a problem in the Improve phase of DMAIC in LSS. Table 7.1 summarizes ways in which TRIZ can be used to enhance the effectiveness of LSS and DFSS. For more detail and power on the TRIZ methodology, we recommend the work of Dr. Michael Slocum and his book on *INsourcing Innovation* (see list of references). Dr. Slocum and others have spent years extending the work of Altshuller to make it as systematic and intuitive as possible.

Note that the Innovation track in Figure 7.6 supports both the Preservation and Evolution domains via LSS and DesIgNNOVATION™, respectively. The tactical part of TRIZ is the part of Innovation that supports the Preservation and LSS area. Innovation also supports the DesIgNNOVATION™ track via both strategic and tactical TRIZ, along with other innovation techniques. Besides having a supporting role in both LSS and DesIgNNOVATION™, our Innovation track has its own curriculum and certification structure independent of LSS and DFSS. The certification criteria are similar to the LSS and DFSS certification criteria given in Chapters 5 and 6, i.e., course work, exams, project completion, and appropriate written and verbal documentation. Clearly, innovation is a critical element of our A^3CE Model as it is used to enhance both the Preservation and Evolution domains of an enterprise.

- *TRIZ can be used to resolve inverse correlation effects in the interaction matrices (or roofs) of the Houses of Quality in QFD.*

- *TRIZ can be used in the Improve phase of DMAIC.*

- *TRIZ can be used to develop alternative design concepts in the conceptual design phase of IDOV (Identify, Design, Optimize, Validate).*

- *Design concepts can then be used in Pugh Concept Selection, and TRIZ can be used to create new designs within the iterative Pugh methodology.*

- *TRIZ can be used in the Optimize phase of IDOV, when the performance of B is degraded while the performance of A is improved, i.e., to resolve these technical contradictions.*

- *TRIZ can be used to resolve contradictions in a transfer function when the input parameters conflict with one another.*

- *TRIZ can also be used in the Optimize phase to introduce new elements to the optimization process, thereby creating a more open optimization space vis-à-vis a closed optimization space.*

Table 7.1 Integration of TRIZ into LSS and DFSS

We define innovation as the act of introducing or discovering something new or creative. Historically, it has been perceived to be the product of eureka moments. It is something organizations desperately want and need but can't seem to define or get. Innovation has become a key buzzword in the marketplace. One cannot read **Business Week**, **Time**, **Newsweek** or any other periodical, technical or not, without seeing or hearing about innovation. Consequently, there are myriad meanings of innovation invading the marketplace. Evidence of this is shown by even the university system getting engaged with innovation. The University of Colorado at Colorado Springs is trying to gain approval from the University of Colorado Board of Regents to start a Bachelors of Innovation (BI) degree (**Colorado Springs Gazette Telegraph**, 31 Oct 06). It remains to be seen whether their curriculum will include DFSS, TRIZ, and other innovative techniques mentioned in this text. However, Keeping Innovation Systematic and Simple (KISS) is the approach we are taking in our Innovation track of the A^{3}CE Model.

Our belief is that the systematic practice of innovation is necessary for the continued viability of any organization. It is no longer acceptable to bet the future of a company on unpredictable epiphanies or on a sequence of trials and errors to produce something meaningful. We know that innovation must take place in the crevices between disciplines, i.e., it must be interdisciplinary as well as multidisciplinary. We also know that innovation can be reduced to the application of algorithms and scientific principles and that it can be absorbed by anyone in any organization, be they left-brained or right-brained. The TRIZ methodology and related analytical methods, including statistical thinking, form the core of our systematic innovation practice. This approach allows the application of innovation to produce results predictably, reliably, and repeatably.

Innovation, then, no longer has to remain a scarce resource but rather can become a renewable one that can be systematically leveraged for problem solving and ideation. When implemented organization-wide, our systematic and simple–and thus powerful–approach to innovation becomes the cornerstone of sustained economic viability.

We present a final set of knowledge generating questions. These are **Questions Leaders Must Answer** in order to assess where they are on their journey to competitive excellence. Table 7.2 lists these questions which provide a knowledge generating strategy for competitive excellence. They should remind leaders that competitive excellence doesn't just happen. It must be built into the business strategy, planned, deployed, executed, and assessed just like the other knowledge generating strategies presented in Chapters 4 - 6.

---

1. *Are both the Voice of the Customer (VOC) and Societal Needs (or Voice of Society—VOS) built into the knowledge based strategic plan? Furthermore, do we have a systematic approach to measure the mood of the marketplace so that we understand the VOC and can anticipate the VOS? Show the data that supports the answer to this question.*

2. *What is the current bias between the Preservation and Evolution states of our business and what resources have been allocated to each? Show the data that supports the answer to this question.*

(Continued on Next Page)

Table 7.2 Questions Leaders Must Answer in Competitive Excellence

3. *What knowledge generating strategies are we currently using to support the Preservation and Evolution states? And what impact have they had on our business scorecard? Show the supporting data.*

4. *What are the short-term and long-term plans for shifting the bias between Preservation (VOC) and Evolution (VOS)? What does the current trend say? Show the supporting data.*

5. *Have we aligned the knowledge generating improvement methods with the business strategy and properly allocated the required resources? Support your answer with data.*

6. *What is our plan to improve the knowledge and capabilities of all employees so that each person can contribute to the competitive excellence of our organization? What percentage of our employee base is directly supporting competitive excellence? What percentage will be supporting competitive excellence one year from now?*

7. *What is our company's innovation agenda and what is expected of our leaders to support this agenda? Can we identify the efforts that show how our innovation agenda is being accomplished?*

Table 7.2 Questions Leaders Must Answer in Competitive Excellence

There is no single methodology today that can serve all possible needs. That is why a competitive excellence strategy, like the A^{3}CE Model, that incorporates multiple knowledge generating strategies, is the optimal strategy to pursue. We hope this chapter has given you a vision of a bigger picture that will help you accommodate and align all of your improvement efforts. Achieving and maintaining competitive excellence is a journey, not an end state. We hope this text will help you no matter where you find yourself on the competitive excellence continuum of gaining knowledge.

> *"Knowledge has to be improved, challenged, and increased constantly, or it vanishes."*
>
> *Peter Drucker*

Appendix

DMAIC Projects and Results

- Reduction in Oil Well Production Downtime   ($2.5 M)

- Improved Automatic Well Testing Process   ($500 K)

- Water Treatment Process Improvement   ($854 K)

- Pharmacist Information Outsert Improvement   ($4 M)

- Reduction in Crankshaft Production Failures   ($100 K)

- Reduction in Engineering Parts Design
  Cycle Time by 45%

- Reduction of Machine Downtime on Packaging   ($90 K)

- Reduced Variation in Alumina Refinery
  Titration Process   ($180 K)

- Improved Production Rates and Reduced
  Losses of Methyl Ethyl Katone (MEK)
  and Ethanol   ($25 M)

- Submersible Pump Repair Process
  Improvement   ($437 K)

- Fleet Vehicle Maintenance Cost Reduction   ($1.8 M)

- TV Deflection Yoke Design Upgrade   ($964 K)

- Improved Property Management System
  (over 4 years)   ($11M)
    - Prevented Customer Disapproval of the Property
      System
    - Property Held Due to Errors Reduced by 67%
    - Reduced Material Movement by 28 Miles
    - Reduced Cycle Time by 80%

- Credit/Billing Process Improvements   ($69 K)

- Space Consolidation Thru Value Stream Alignment
  (69% Space Reduction)

- Reduction of Energy Demand/Use   ($450 K)

- Mailroom Process Improvements
    - Reduced Floor Space Requirements by 39%
    - Reduced Cycle Time by 63%
    - Reduced Transportation and Queue Length by 68%

- Reduction of Excessive and Redundant IT Applications   ($775 K)

- Reduction in Paid Absences   ($45 K)

- Employee Recruitment Process Improvement   ($67 K)

- Prioritize, Delete, and Delay Indirect Material and Laboratory
  Expense Orders (over 4 years—multiple projects)   ($11 M)

- Improved Accounts Receivable Process
  (outstanding invoices decreased from $7M to under $1M)

- Compensation / Bonus Process Definition Improvement   ($349 K)

- Improved Master Scheduling Process
    - MRP Accuracy Improved to 97%
    - Master Scheduling Cycle Time Reduced from 32 days to 7 days
    - Eliminated Unnecessary Expediting
    - Reduced Staffing Level from 12 to 9

- Improved Employee Productivity When Employees Transfer Jobs within Same Company   ($479 K)

- Improved Time Sheet Accuracy   ($25 K)

- Reduction in Food Service Subsidy   ($60 K)

- Redesign of System for Tracking Defective Material   ($118 K)

- Reduction in Annual Telecommunication Costs   ($500 K)

- Improved Small Business Loan Process   ($1.4 M)

- Improved Credit Underwriting Process   ($6.6 M)

- Improved Customer Service Warranty Claims Process   ($100 K)

- Reduction in Travel Cost Process   ($410 K)

- Improved Accuracy and On-Time Delivery of Drawings   ($292 K)

- Improved Procurement System   ($275 K)

- Artificial Knee Joint Polishing   ($309 K)

- Reduction in Number and Cost of Audits ($454 K)

- Improved Water Quality and Handling ($650 K)

- Reduced Plastic Part Defectives ($246 K)

- Improved Accuracy of Claim Payments ($578 K)

- Pick to Box Process Optimization ($1.94 M)

- Part Washing Process Improvement ($58 K)

- Improved Water Quality ($950 K)

- Minimized Claim Liability ($930 K)

- Coil Winding Process for Spinal Stimulation ($430 K)

- Corona Fan Test Failure Reduction ($280 K)

- Reduced Leakage of Seal ($41 K)

- Process Induced Damage Reduction ($963 K)

- Radiology Set Up Process Improvement ($624 K)

- Reduced Cost of Former Members ($1.02 M)

- Sampling Plan Improvement ($40 K)

- Shutter Spring Optimization DOE ($150 K)

- Reduced PCB Test Failures   ($50 K)

- Dimension PTB Box Marking   ($120 K)

- Reduction in Loop Mail/Missent Mail   ($125 K)

- Reduction in Manual Mail Handling   ($86 K)

- Redefining the Change Management Process During Production (2 projects)   ($347 K)

- Photo Cathode Fabrication Yield Improvement   ($1.01 M)

- Reduction in Sick Leave at 8 Sites   ($2.84 M)

- GPS Navigation System Breakout Box Initiative Proposal Process Improvement   ($130 K)

- HVAC Refrigerant Leak Reduction   ($152 K)

- Employee Turnover Reduction   ($141 K)

- Flat Screen Defect Reduction/Elimination   ($3.65 M)

Glossary

Affinity Diagram: A technique for organizing individual pieces of information into groups or broader categories.

Attribute Data: Data that can be divided into various groups or categories on the basis of some non-numerical characteristics. This term is often used to describe data reflecting conformance or non-conformance to specifications, including observation of the presence or absence of some quality characteristic.

Average: A measure of the central tendency of a sample or population. Synonymous with mean, it is usually denoted by $\bar{y}$ (sample mean) or μ (population mean).

Axiomatic Design (AD): Developed by Dr. Nam Suh at MIT, AD is a systematic design methodology that transforms customer needs into key functional requirements, design parameters, and process variables. The method is based on design axioms or principles which drive the decision making process in developing high quality product designs.

Bell Curve: A bell shaped curve that graphically describes the probability distribution for "normal" data; also called a normal distribution or Gaussian distribution.

Benchmarking: An activity which encompasses the search for and implementation of best practices.

Benefit/Effort Graph: This is a two-dimensional graph with the dimensions labeled "benefit" and "effort." It is used to help prioritize items such as projects in a Lean Six Sigma effort with regard to the benefit to be achieved versus the effort that will have to be expended.

Biological S-Curve: This s-shaped curve describes the natural life cycle of a product or service, from concept to birth, then through adolescence to maturity and then in decline from obsolescence to death.

Black Belt: A key person who is trained to execute critical projects and deliver breakthrough enhancements to the bottom line; also known as an expert or change agent.

Bottleneck: The rate limiting step of a process when demand exceeds capacity. Continually improving the performance of the bottleneck should improve the output of the whole operation until it has been elevated to the point where it is no longer the rate limiting step.

Brainstorming: A group technique used to generate many ideas about a specific topic, issue or solution. It is particularly good at inspiring creativity and synergy between the participants.

Capability (of a CTC or process performance measure): A comparison of the Voice of the Process (VOP), which is given in terms of a data distribution, with the Voice of the Customer (VOC), which is given in terms of specifications. Capability indexes include σ rating, C_p, C_{pk}, dpm.

Cause and Effect Diagram (CE): A pictorial tool that is used to categorize, display and examine potential causes or contributing factors (inputs) related to a specific observed condition (output). This tool is also known as a fishbone diagram or an Ishikawa diagram.

Cavespeak: The dialect used by Citizens Against Virtually Everything (CAVE) people when referring to readiness for change in an organization.

Champion: A senior leader or manager who serves as a deployment leader or project sponsor or process owner within the Lean Six Sigma or Design for Six Sigma strategic rollout.

Changeover: All of the activities associated with switching the materials, operating settings or tooling on a piece of equipment so that it can produce a different part or perform a different task. Changeover time is usually defined as the time elapsed between the production of the last good part of one batch until the first good part of the next batch is produced.

Common Cause Variation: The sources of variability in a process that are truly random and occur naturally as an inherent part of the process.

Common Sense: The demonstration and application of traits shown to be associated with critical thinking and good judgment.

Competitive Excellence: A term used to describe a state of competence of an organization; it means the organization has the ability to survive the current demands of the marketplace and evolve itself to a state of continued and expanded success. It also refers to the initiative of pursuing this state of excellence through a knowledge based strategy, synchronizing the business, and enhancing its intellectual capital using the best of the best improvement methods.

Continuous Variable: A variable that is derived from measurement data (time, weight, pressure, linear measure, etc.) and is considered to have an infinite number of possible values.

Control (of a process): A process is considered to be in a state of statistical control with respect to a specific performance measure when it exhibits only random (common cause) variation. A controlled process is consistent and predictable, but the state of control does not imply anything about the capability of the process or its output.

Control Chart: The most powerful tool of statistical process control. It consists of a run chart, together with statistically determined upper and lower control limits and a centerline.

Control Limits: Upper and lower bounds in a control chart that are determined by the process itself. They can be used to detect special causes of variation. They are usually set at ±3 standard deviations from the center line which is usually the mean.

Correlation Coefficient: A measure of the linear relationship between two variables. Correlation does not imply causality.

Cost of Doing Nothing (CODN): The cost of maintaining the status quo when no formalized improvement efforts are undertaken. It includes the Cost of Poor Quality and the Cost of Waste.

Cost of Poor Quality (COPQ): The cost of the "waste" associated with all of the processes (administrative and production oriented) within a business. This includes costs related to internal and external failures, appraisal, prevention and lost opportunities. Often associated with any activity related to not doing the right thing right the first time.

C_p: A process capability index defined as the ratio of specification width (USL - LSL) to process width (6σ).

C_{pk}: During process capability studies C_{pk} is an index used to compare the natural tolerances of a process with the specification limits. If C_{pk} is negative, the process mean is outside the specification limits; if C_{pk} is between 0 and 1, then the natural tolerances of the process fall outside the spec limits. If C_{pk} is larger than 1, the natural tolerances fall completely within the spec limits. A value of 1.5 or greater is usually desired.

Creativity: The ability to produce new, innovative products and services.

Critical to Customer (CTC): A measure of process or product performance that is related to customer requirements or customer satisfaction; it is usually associated with timeliness (speed), quality (accuracy), or cost; a CTC must be measurable. Also referred to as a CTQ (Critical to Quality).

Customer: Anyone who uses or consumes a product or service, whether internal or external to the providing organization or provider.

Customer Needs and Expectations: Customer wants, desires, wishes, and demands for products and services translated into measurable indicators of cost, quality (various dimensions), and delivery (time and quantity). Often referred to as customer requirements.

Customer Retention Grid: Introduced by Dr. Tom Connellan, it is a two-dimensional grid using both "process" and "outcome" dimensions to categorize the state of the customer. It also shows that customer satisfaction does not equate to customer loyalty.

Customer Value: The degree of worth in usefulness and importance that a customer places on a product or service that he uses or is exposed to. It is usually dependent on cost, speed (timeliness) and quality (useful, reliable, accurate).

Cycle Time: The elapsed time for a product to progress completely through its process, i.e., from the start of the first step until the end of the last step. The term cycle time can also be applied to an operator or a piece of equipment. Operator cycle time is the time required for an operator to complete the full sequence of his or her assigned tasks and return to the start position. Similarly, equipment cycle time is the time required for a machine to complete the full sequence of operations associated with its production task.

D1-9000: An aerospace industry (Boeing specific) standard for documenting quality improvement systems, to include the proper use of statistical tools.

DCOV: A 4-phase Design for Six Sigma strategy: Design, Characterize, Optimize, Validate.

Defects per Million (dpm): A capability measure which describes the number of defective units per million units produced.

Design for Six Sigma (DFSS): An improvement strategy which is particularly useful during the early phases of the product or service development cycle with the intention of reducing variability and "designing the quality in" rather than improving the process or product later.

Design of Experiments (DOE): An organized method of collecting data by purposefully changing the process inputs in order to observe and measure the corresponding changes in the process output. DOE provides a method to develop powerful empirical models which approximate the true relationships between various process inputs and the output. Understanding these relationships allows us to improve the process performance characteristics.

DesIgNNOVATION™: A term in competitive excellence that comprises DFSS and Innovation, along with all the tools and techniques that support these methodologies.

DFLSS: Design for Lean Six Sigma. As used herein, a variant of DFSS.

DFSS Capability Maturity Model: A 2-dimensional grid used to assess maturity in a DFSS rollout.

DFSS Scorecard: The repository of the cumulative body of knowledge regarding a design of a product or service. It is broken down into segments such as parts, process, performance, and software.

Discrete Variable: A variable that is based upon "count" data (the number of defects, the number of births, the number of units produced, etc.). In some cases the counts may be very large, but they are finite and considered to be "countable."

Dispersion of a Sample: The tendency of the values in a data set to differ from each other. Dispersion is commonly expressed in terms of the range of the sample (difference between the lowest and highest values) or by the standard deviation.

DMADV: A 5-phase Design for Six Sigma strategy: Define, Measure, Analyze, Design, Verify.

DMAIC: The standard Six Sigma and Lean Six Sigma phased approach to project execution: Define, Measure, Analyze, Improve, Control.

Error Proofing (Poka-yoke): A series of techniques which are used to reduce the opportunity for errors to occur.

Evolution: The competitive excellence domain focused on the development of new products and services; the ability of an organization to recreate itself by developing new life cycle curves. It is driven by the Voice of Society (or societal needs).

Expected Value Analysis (EVA): A term used in DFSS to describe the process of predicting what the output of a process will be (shape, mean, and standard deviation) when using only the transfer function and the input variables' distributions.

Experimental Design: Specifically, it is purposeful changes to the inputs (factors) of a process in order to observe corresponding changes in the outputs (responses). Also known as DOE.

Failure Mode and Effect Analysis (FMEA): A tool which is used to systematically identify, analyze, prioritize (on basis of a risk assessment) and reduce or eliminate potential process or product failure modes.

Fault Tree Analysis (FTA): A technique for evaluating the possible causes which might lead to the failure of a product. For each possible failure, the possible causes of the failure are determined; then the situations leading to those causes are determined; and so forth, until all paths leading to possible failures have been traced. The result is a flow chart for the failure process. Plans to deal with each path can then be made.

Fishbone Diagram: See cause and effect diagram.

Flow: The movement of a product or service through each of its process steps.

Flowchart: A graphic representation that symbolically shows the sequential activities and branching in a process that produces an output.

FOCUS: An acronym for a 5-step breakdown of the PDCA cycle's planning phase. Find a process to improve. Organize a team. Clarify current knowledge. Understand causes of variation. Select the process improvement that we plan to do.

Frontier Model: A partitioned normal curve that describes the approximate percentages of people in an organization who are in various states of readiness for change: Pioneers, Settlers, CAVE people.

Gage Capability Study: Collecting data to assess how much variation is in the measurement system itself and to compare it to the total process variation. Also more generically referred to as Measurement System Analysis.

Green Belt: A person trained to provide technical assistance to a Black Belt and/or undertake projects of lesser scope than a Black Belt project; also known as a specialist or associate.

Hidden Factory: The set of activities and processes that are devoted to rework, scrap and waste, i.e., not doing the right things right the very first time. It is where the COPQ and Waste exist in an organization.

Histogram: A vertical bar graph which illustrates the distribution of numerical data according to the frequency of occurrence within defined value ranges (classes).

ICOV: A 4-phase Design for Six Sigma strategy: Identify, Characterize, Optimize, Validate.

Ideation: The process of defining the ideal final state of a system or product.

IDOV: The original 4-phase Design for Six Sigma strategy: Identify, Design, Optimize, Validate.

Innovation: The act of discovering and introducing something new or creative that satisfies a societal need.

Input Process Output (IPO) Diagram: A visual representation of a process where inputs are represented by input arrows to a box (which represents the process) and outputs are shown using arrows emanating out of the box.

Ishikawa Diagram: See Cause and Effect Diagram.

ISO-9000: An international standard for documenting quality assurance systems.

Just In Time (JIT): A manufacturing strategy which strives to rapidly respond to the pull of the customer and to reduce inventories by producing the exact number of units required at the right time with no waste and continuous flow.

Kaikaku: Radical improvement or transformation of an activity to reduce or eliminate waste.

Kaizen: Continuous small (incremental) improvements in an activity over time which reduce waste.

Kanban: A Japanese term which means "card signal." However, this term is often used more generally to describe any visual signal used to indicate the need for material replenishment by an upstream activity.

Kirkpatrick's Model: A 4-tiered model that describes the various ways that the effect of training can be measured: like, learn, use, and financial return.

KISS: Keep It Simple Statistically. Also Keeping Innovation Systematic and Simple.

Knowledge Based Management (KBM): A leadership and management philosophy predicated on good decision making which emphasizes the use of knowledge and data rather than opinion and perception. It is composed of three elements: the Questions Leaders Need to Answer, Questions Leaders Need to Ask, and the improvement strategies described in this text that are needed to generate and deliver the right knowledge to the right people at the right time.

Lean: The continuous elimination of unnecessary, non-value added steps (or waste) within a process or value stream. It is also an improvement strategy that embraces two primary principles: flow and pull.

Lean Production: The principal philosophy of lean production is the elimination of waste, particularly as defined by the 7 types of waste. However, in a broader context, lean production refers to many of the techniques and methods described in this text which contribute to the company's ability to respond quickly and efficiently to customer demand by delivering high quality products when and where needed.

Lean Six Sigma: A business philosophy and improvement strategy which combines the strategies of Lean (reduction of waste and queue times) and Six Sigma (reduction of variation). These concepts must be applied to all facets of the business in order to achieve a truly "lean enterprise."

Little's Law: A mathematical expression that describes the relationship between key terms used in capacity analysis: Cycle Time = (Work in Process)/Throughput.

Load Chart: A vertical bar chart which compares the workload, in units of time, assigned to each operator or piece of equipment in a work cell. The cycle times within the cell should be balanced so that they are approximately equal, thereby minimizing idle time and delays. The overall process cycle time should be equal to the Takt Time.

Lower Specification Limit (LSL): The lowest value of a product dimension or measurement which is acceptable. Represents the VOC.

Master Black Belt: A full-time resource who is both a technical mentor for Black Belts and Green Belts and also an internal consultant and trainer.

Matrix: A graphic that is used to show the relationship between two or more groups of characteristics, ideas, or issues.

Mean: The average of a set of values. We usually use $\bar{x}$ or $\bar{y}$ to denote a sample mean, and we use the Greek letter μ to denote a population mean. See Average. Graphically, it is the balance point for a set of data.

Measurement System Analysis (MSA): A statistical technique that quantifies the amount of the variability that originates from the measurement system itself. In this context, the measurement system includes the operator and process/equipment used to perform the measurement.

Median: The middle value of a data set when the values are arranged in either ascending or descending order.

Metric: A performance measure that is considered to be a key pulse point of an organization. It should be linked to goals or objectives and carefully monitored.

Mission: A statement defining an organization's unique purpose.

Modeling Design: A type of designed experiment whose primary purpose is to build a mathematical model that characterizes the relationship between key input factors and a critical response variable.

Muda: Any activity which is wasteful, i.e., it uses time or resources, but does not add any value from the perspective of the customer. The Japanese word for waste.

Multiple Regression: A mathematical modeling methodology where several independent variables are used to predict the value of a dependent variable. Can be used to develop transfer functions.

Natural Tolerances of a Process: 3 standard deviations on either side of the center point (mean value). In a stable, normally distributed process, the natural tolerances encompass 99.73% of all measurements.

Non-Value Added (NVA): Activities which consume time or resources but do not directly contribute towards meeting the customer's requirements.

Normal Distribution: A probability distribution, also known as the Gaussian distribution, which is graphically represented by a smooth bell shaped curve.

Out of Control: A process is said to be out of control if it exhibits variation beyond its control limits or shows a systematic pattern of variation.

Outlier: A data point which is very unusual when compared to the rest of the data set.

Output: A product produced or a service delivered by a process. It is often measured in terms of the quantity and quality of product or service delivered that meets a certain requirement, such as cost, quality (dimensions), and delivery (time and quantity) requirements.

Paradigm: A set of boundaries (perhaps consciously, subconsciously, or even unconsciously defined) that form the limits of behavior, opinions, and decision-making.

Parameter Design: A term used in DFSS that refers to the process of finding the most optimal location parameters (means) of the input variable distributions in order to maximize output capability; sometimes referred to as robust design.

Pareto Chart: A vertical bar chart that relates various attribute (non-numerical) categories to their respective cost or frequency of occurrence. Bars are presented in descending order.

PCOR: A 4-phase strategy for performance improvement: Prioritize, Characterize, Optimize and Realize.

PDCA: The Plan-Do-Check-Act cycle (also known as the Shewhart or Deming cycle) is a repeatable four-phase implementation strategy for process improvement.

PF/CE/CNX/SOP: A management philosophy and methodology that is used to reduce extraneous variation. It uses Process Flow (PF) diagrams and Cause and Effect (CE) diagrams to identify and sort the causes of variation. The causes are further categorized as Controllable ("C"), Noise ("N") or eXperimental ("X"). Standard operating procedures (SOPs) are used to establish methods for changing the "N" variables into "C" variables.

Physical Process Map: A layout diagram of the work area that illustrates the path followed by materials or parts through the facility. It can be used to highlight excessive amounts of material transport or employee movement while following the steps described in a process flow chart. Synonymous with spaghetti diagram.

Poka-Yoke: Any technique which is used to reduce the likelihood of an error (e.g., color coding unique design characteristics which prevent improper assembly). These techniques are best applied in the design phase of a process to prevent errors but can also be implemented as a corrective action to prevent recurrence of an error.

Preservation: The competitive excellence domain that focuses on maintaining or protecting the current market position of a business; it includes maintaining market share, profitability, and brand recognition. It is driven by the Voice of the Customer.

Probability Distribution: A table, graph or formula that describes the probabilities of all of the possible outcomes of a process. Many naturally occurring phenomena and processes can be described by a probability distribution. Knowing the characteristics of the distribution that is associated with a specific experiment, process, or phenomenon allows us to make accurate predictions regarding the likelihood of certain events related to that experiment, process or phenomenon. Data sets tend to follow certain distributions.

Process: An activity which blends a set of inputs for the purpose of producing a product, providing a service, or performing a task.

Process Capability: Comparing actual process performance (VOP) with process specification limits (VOC). There are various measures of process capability, such as C_p, C_{pk}, dpm (defects per million), and σ Rating.

Process Characterization: Demonstrating the ability to thoroughly understand a process, to include the specific relationship between the outputs and the inputs of a process.

Process Control: A process is said to be in control or it is a stable, predictable process if all special causes of variation have been removed. Only common causes or natural variation remain in the process.

Process Control Chart: A fundamental tool of Statistical Process Control (SPC) which is used to determine if a process is statistically under control, i.e., stable and predictable within the bounds of natural variation.

Process Flow and Control System (PFCS): The system of interacting methods, tools, techniques, reporting procedures, and feedback that controls the critical parameters and variables in a process or value stream in order to maintain optimal performance.

Process Flow Diagram: See flowchart.

Process Observation Chart: A table used to record specific attributes of each step while carefully watching the process. The attributes of interest usually include the type of process step (e.g., operation, transport, inspection, waiting, storage or decision), quantity, distance and elapsed time.

Process Validation: Establishing documented evidence which provides a high degree of assurance that a specific process will consistently produce a product that meets its pre-determined specifications and quality characteristics.

Project: Refers to the work effort required to successfully complete the entire set of phases or tollgates in executing the LSS (DMAIC) or DFSS (IDOV) methodology.

Pugh Concept Selection: A design methodology originated by Stuart Pugh that is used in iterative fashion to derive a best final design or designs. It can also be used independently of the design process as a decision matrix.

Pull Production: A production strategy which requires downstream process steps to signal a need for replenishment before activity in each of the previous (upstream) process steps is initiated. In the ideal pull system, no production begins until the customer purchases the product, and even then, it is only produced in the quantity consumed. The customer demand "pulls" the product through the process.

Push Production: A batch and queue production strategy which produces product by controlling the input, i.e., the "front end" of the process. When orders are placed on the system, often based on forecast rather than true customer demand, batch production is initiated at the first step to meet and usually exceed the demand.

QS-9000: A U.S. automotive industry standard for documenting quality improvement systems, to include the proper use of statistical tools.

Quality Function Deployment (QFD): A systematic process used to integrate customer requirements into every aspect of the design and delivery of products and services.

Quality Systems Review (QSR): Motorola's standard for documenting quality improvement systems, to include the proper use of statistical tools.

Random Sample: A sample drawn from the population in such a way that every element of the population has an equally likely chance of being selected.

Range: A measure of the variability or "spread" of a data set. It is the difference between the maximum and minimum values in the data set.

Rapid Improvement Event (RIE): A quick hitting improvement effort that should not last longer than 5 days. Within a LSS (DMAIC) project, it is usually part of the Improve phase. Also known as a Kaizen event or a PF/CE/CNX/SOP effort.

Regression Analysis: See Multiple Regression.

Requirements Flowdown: The process of translating customer requirements into a prioritized list of functional requirements and then further into prioritized design parameters and process parameters. Quality Function Deployment (QFD) and Axiomatic Design (AD) are methods that can be used to accomplish this.

Return on Investment (ROI): A metric that is used to gauge the success of an initiative like LSS or DFSS, or projects or studies within these improvement strategies. It is usually measured in percentage of the original financial investment or in percentage of the revenue or budget.

Rework: Activity required to correct for defects produced by a process.

Robust Design: A term used in design engineering that means making the output variables or response measures insensitive to variability in the input variables.

Rule of Thumb (ROT): A simplified, practical procedure that can be used in place of a formal method and will produce approximately the same result.

Run Chart: A basic graphical tool that charts a process over time, recording either individual readings, averages, ranges, standard deviations, etc., over time.

Scatter Diagram: A chart in which one variable is plotted against another to determine if there is a correlation between the two variables.

Screening Design: A type of designed experiment whose primary purpose is to separate the significant factors from the insignificant factors.

Seven Types of Waste: Delineated by Taiichi Ohno at Toyota, these seven types of waste are found in all types of manufacturing and transactional/service processes: Transportation, Inventory, Motion, Waiting, Over-production, Over-processing, Defects (TIMWOOD).

Sigma: A Greek letter (σ) used to represent the standard deviation of a population of data.

Sigma Level: A commonly used measure of process capability that represents the number of standard deviations between the process center (the mean) and the nearest specification limit. Also known as a Z - value.

Single Minute Exchange of Dies (SMED): A series of techniques used to facilitate the rapid changeover of any process or equipment.

Single Piece Flow: A production strategy in which units progress individually (as a batch of one unit) through each of its associated process steps with continuous flow in the forward direction (i.e., without rework). It can be contrasted with the batch and queue strategy in which batches of multiple units proceed as a group through each of the production steps. This procedure requires each unit to "stop and wait" for each of the other units in the batch to be completed before the group proceeds to the next process step.

Six Sigma: A performance improvement and business strategy that began in the 1980's at Motorola. Emphasis is on reducing defects, reducing cycle time with aggressive goals, and reducing costs to dramatically impact the bottom line. It involves establishing an organizational infrastructure together with a repeatable methodology and tools to accomplish business objectives.

Six Sigma Barrier: The barrier existing at 4 - 5 sigma capability that is apparent in almost all LSS projects is due to the underlying design of the product or service. DFSS can be used to push this barrier back so that there is financial incentive to move toward the higher levels of capability.

SMART Goals: Project goals should be SMART: Specific, Measurable, Achievable, Relevant, and Timely.

Societal Needs (Voice of Society): These are the drivers of the Evolution domain of competitive excellence, because customers will not be able to relate what they want 3-10 years downstream.

Special Cause Variation: Non-random causes of variation that can be detected by the use of control charts and good process documentation. A process is said to be in a state of statistical control when all sources of special cause variation have been eliminated.

Specification Limits: The bounds of acceptable performance for a given product or process. They represent the VOC.

Standard Deviation: A commonly used measure of variability or "spread" in a data set or population. It is equal to the square root of the variance.

Standard Operating Procedure (SOP): An up-to-date written procedure that clearly and concisely describes the exact method to be followed in order to complete a specific task.

Standard Work: A method of improving work efficiency and reducing variability by ensuring that everyone follows exactly the same procedure to complete a specific task. The procedure may be improved as new ideas or technology become available. However, the modified procedure must first be demonstrated to be superior and if adopted as the best practice, everyone who is performing that task must follow it.

Statistical Process Control (SPC): The use of basic graphical and statistical methods for measuring, analyzing, and controlling the variation of a process for the purpose of continuously improving the process.

Stretch Goal: A goal not easily attainable, yet not impossible, designed to create out-of-the box thinking to achieve breakthrough improvement.

Study: This is an effort that is smaller in scope than a project. A study is the application of a tool or methodology that provides immediate knowledge for the purpose of gaining quick successes. A study does not complete the entire tollgate phases of DMAIC or IDOV.

Survey: A means of gathering data on people, processes, products, and organizations. It is usually accomplished via questionnaires, interviews, etc.

Takt Time: The average time to produce a unit in order to meet the current rate of customer demand.

Teamwork: Cooperative effort on the part of members of a group or team to achieve a common goal.

Time Value Map: A time scaled graph that illustrates the amount of active and inactive time spent during one complete cycle of a process.

Tolerance Allocation: A term used in DFSS that refers to the process of finding which input variables' standard deviations must be reduced and which ones can be allowed to expand; also referred to as tolerance design.

Tolerances: This is the acceptable or permissible deviation from a specific target value of a CTC or performance measure.

Total Productive Maintenance (TPM): A comprehensive and coordinated maintenance program designed to maximize equipment effectiveness by minimizing downtime and optimizing output in terms of speed and quality. This approach is founded upon the ability of well trained equipment operators to proactively identify and correct small maintenance issues before they become significant and lead to breakdowns.

Total Quality Management (TQM): A management philosophy of integrated controls, including engineering, purchasing, financial administration, marketing and manufacturing, to ensure customer satisfaction and economical cost of quality.

Transfer Function: This is a mathematical relationship between a response variable (y) and one or more input or predictor variables (x's).

Trend: A gradual, systematic change over time or some other variable.

TRIZ: In Russian, Teoriya Resheniya Izobretatelskikh Zadatch, which translated into English means Theory of Inventive Problem Solving. Developed by Genrich Altshuller, TRIZ is an innovative problem solving methodology that converges on the solution(s) rather than promoting divergent thought processes for innovation.

Upper Specification Limit (USL): The highest value of a product dimension or measurement which is acceptable. Represents the VOC.

Value: Some feature, condition, service or product that the customer considers desirable and which is delivered to them when and where they want it.

Value Stream: All of the activities which are performed to transform a product or service into what is required by the customer.

Value Stream Mapping: A diagram which describes all of the activities in a product value stream.

Variability: A generic term that refers to the property of a metric (or key measurement) to take on different values.

Variables: Metrics or performance measures which are subject to change or variability.

Variables Data: A measurement whose value is only limited by the sensitivity and resolution of the measuring system. Opposite of attribute data.

Variance: A specifically defined mathematical measure of variability in a data set or population. It is the square of the standard deviation.

Variation: See variability.

Vision: Ideals, hopes, and dreams that bring meaning to what we do. It provides the reason for an organization's being.

Visual Management: A series of visual techniques which are used to communicate the status of a system in such a way that it can be understood at a glance by everyone concerned. The term "system" is used broadly to describe everything from simple conditions such as the presence or absence of the tools required to perform a specific task (e.g., a changeover system), or more complex operations such as graphs reporting key performance indicators for a business.

Voice of the Customer (VOC): A term which describes any method of collecting information about what is important to the customer. It includes but is not limited to: customer specifications, customer design requirements, customer surveys and listening to customer feedback. When capability is computed, VOC is represented by specifications.

Voice of the Process (VOP): A term which refers to the data collected on a specific Critical-to-Customer (CTC) performance measure. When capability is computed, VOP is represented by a data distribution.

Waste: Any activity or process that does not add value to the product from the perspective of the customer.

Waste Analysis: An examination of a process that is conducted to identify and separate value added activities from non-value added activities (waste).

Work Cell: A work area, often including machines, which has been designed to facilitate production activities by one or more operators. The physical layout and activities in a cell are very organized and carefully sequenced to optimize flow of materials with minimal effort.

Work Cell Design: A technique used to develop the optimal physical layout of the work area to improve the worker's ability to maximize product throughput and quality.

Work In Process (WIP): Material which has been partially processed, but has not yet reached the state of approved finished product.

Yield: The proportion of "good" units produced (output) relative to the theoretical maximum number of units which could be produced on the basis of material input quantities. Yield is usually expressed as a percentage of theoretical maximum, but is also sometimes described in terms of absolute quantities (e.g., kilograms of product).

Z-value: A standardized value calculated by subtracting the mean and then dividing this difference by the standard deviation. It represents the number of standard deviations between a specified value and the mean.

References and Resources

Adams, Kiemele, Pollock and Quan. *Lean Six Sigma: A Tools Guide, 2nd Edition*. Air Academy Associates, Colorado Springs, CO, 2004.

Bossidy, Larry and Charam, Ram. *Execution-The Discipline of Getting Things Done*. Crown Business, New York, NY, 2002.

Carnegie, Dale. *How to Win Friends and Influence People*. Pocket Books, 1981.

Collins, Jim. *Good to Great*. Harper Business, New York, NY, 2001.

CTQ Media LLC. iSixSigma Internet Portal (www.isixsigma.com). Michael Cyger, Publisher.

CTQ Media LLC. *iSixSigma Magazine*, published bi-monthly. Michael Cyger, Publisher.

CTQ Media LLC. RealInnovation Internet Portal (www.RealInnovation.com). Michael Cyger, Publisher.

Deming, W. Edwards. *Out of the Crisis*. MIT Center for Advanced Engineering Study, Cambridge, MA, 1986.

Digital Computations. DFSS Master Monte Carlo Simulation Software Using Microsoft ® Excel. Six Sigma Products Group, Colorado Springs, CO.

Digital Computations. SimWare PRO Simulation Software. Six Sigma Products Group, Colorado Springs, CO.

Digital Computations and Air Academy Associates. DOE PRO XL Design of Experiments Software Using Microsoft ® Excel. Six Sigma Products Group, Colorado Springs, CO.

Digital Computations and Air Academy Associates. SPC XL Statistical Software Using Microsoft ® Excel. Six Sigma Products Group, Colorado Springs, CO.

Domb, Ellen and Rantanen, Kalevi. *Simplified TRIZ*. CRC Press LLC, Boca Raton, FL, 2002.

Gates, Bill. *Business @ The Speed of Thought.* Warner Books, New York, NY, 1999.

George, Michael. *Lean Six Sigma.* McGraw-Hill, New York, NY, 2002.

Hopp, Wallace J. and Spearman, Mark L. *Factory Physics, 2nd Edition.* McGraw-Hill, New York, NY, 2001.

Hutton, David W. *The Change Agents' Handbook: A Survival Guide for Quality Improvement Champions.* ASQC Quality Press, Milwaukee, WI, 1994.

Ishikawa, Kaoru. *Guide to Quality Control.* Asian Productivity Organization, Tokyo, Japan, 1982.

Ishikawa, Kaoru. *What is Total Quality Control?* Prentice Hall, Englewood Cliffs, NJ, 1985.

Joyner, Bryan. *Fourth Generation Management.* McGraw-Hill, New York, NY, 1994.

Juran, J. M. *Juran on Leadership for Quality.* The Free Press, New York, NY, 1989.

Juran, J. M. *Juran on Planning for Quality.* The Free Press, New York, NY, 1988.

Kaplan, Robert S. and Norton, David P. *The Balanced Scorecard.* Harvard Business School Press, 1996.

Kiemele, Mark J., Schmidt, Stephen R., and Berdine, Ronald J. *Basic Statistics: Tools for Continuous Improvement (4th ed).* Air Academy Associates, Colorado Springs, CO, 1997.

Kotter, John P. *Leading Change.* Harvard Business School Press, 1996.

Lu, David J. *Kanban Just-in-Time at Toyota: Management Begins at the Workplace.* Productivity Press, 1989.

Maxwell, John C. *The 21 Indispensable Qualities of a Leader*.
Thomas Nelson Publishers, Nashville, TN, 1999.

Palmer, Brien. *Making Change Work*. ASQ Quality Press, Milwaukee,
WI, 2004.

Patterson, Kerry and Grenny, Joseph, et al. *Crucial Conversations—
Tools for Talking When Stakes Are High*. McGraw-Hill, New
York, NY, 2002.

Schmidt, Stephen R. and Launsby, Robert G. *Understanding
Industrial Designed Experiments (4th ed)*. Air Academy
Associates, Colorado Springs, CO, 1993.

Sharma, Anand and Moody, Patricia E. *The Perfect Engine*. Free
Press, 2001.

Silverstein, David, DeCarlo, Neil, and Slocum, Michael. *INsourcing
Innovation*. Breakthrough Performance Press, Longmont,
CO, 2005.

Slater, Robert. *Jack Welch and the GE Way*. McGraw-Hill, 1999.

Smith, Dick and Blakeslee, Jerry. *Strategic Six Sigma*. John Wiley &
Sons, Inc., Hoboken, NJ, 2002.

Stamatis, D. H. *Failure Mode and Effect Analysis*. ASQC Quality
Press, 1995.

Walton, Mary. *The Deming Management Method*. The Putnam
Publishing Group, 1986.

Welch, Jack with John A. Byrne. *Jack: Straight from the Gut*. Warner
Business Books, 2001.

Womack, James P. and Jones, Daniel T. *Lean Thinking*. Simon &
Schuster, 1996.

Index